To Dad

Happy

xx

£54x

To Dad

Hap

NORTHUMBERLAND and DURHAM

A Social and Political Miscellany

BY

Frank Graham

1979

Published by Frank Graham, 6 Queen's Terrace, Newcastle upon Tyne NE2 2PL
Printed by Howe Brothers (Gateshead) Limited, Swan Street, Gateshead

I.S.B.N. 085983 113 2

PREFACE

Ten years ago we published a Social Miscellany of Northumberland and Durham. It was followed in 1971 by an Industrial Miscellany. The two books were very successful. We have now published an entirely new book in which the number of illustrations and their variety has almost doubled. We have tried to describe events in our social and political history which are often omitted in more formal books and have relied mainly on illustrations. Some of these are so rare and important that we decided not to use the cheap modern method of lithography but the more expensive letterpress which guarantees almost perfect reproduction. We intend to follow with several similar volumes which we hope to publish at yearly intervals.

ACKNOWLEDGEMENTS

Most of the illustrations are drawn from our own collection but several have been supplied by South Tyneside Public Libraries and Museums, (including all the views and adverts from South Shields not acknowledged in text), Mrs. I. E. Rounthwaite and the Northumberland Record Office.

CONTENTS

NOTICE.

Information having been given that several of the Workmen of South Hetton and Murton Collieries are guilty of playing at Cards, and other sorts of Gambling, on the Sabbath Days; they are hereby required to take Notice, that whoever is detected doing so, will be immediately discharged and further dealt with, according to Law; and the Police have orders to watch strictly, and give the names into the Colliery Office of those who may be found acting in such un-christianlike manner.

THOMAS E. FORSTER, Viewer.

South Hetton Colliery Office, July 15th, 1852.

E. SMITH & SON, PRINTERS, 188, HIGH STREET, SUNDERLAND.

JOSEPH CRAWHALL *1821-1896*

Newcastle has produced two of the greatest of English wood-engravers, Thomas Bewick and Joseph Crawhall. The work of Bewick is internationally recognised but Joseph Crawhall is known only to a small number of people who appreciate the remarkable books he produced during the nineteenth century.

His father was a well established industrialist who owned the St. Anne's Ropery. The rope-shaped brick chimney was his father's design. Joseph Crawhall, Jr. was born at West House, Newcastle, a fine house on the banks of the Tyne. His first book published in 1859 was *The Compleatist*

Angling Booke. This rare and charming book was typical of all the books he published. It was hand made in every sense with antique type and woodcuts in the old style. Crawhall's fame rests on his work as a book designer. Many of them were actually printed by the artist himself.

Crawhall's finest book is probably his *Chap-Book Chaplets* published in 1883, a collection of ballads with hand-coloured illustrations. We recently republished this book in facsimile with paper specially made to resemble the original. This limited edition is an outstanding example of modern facsimile printing.

Advert 1887

4

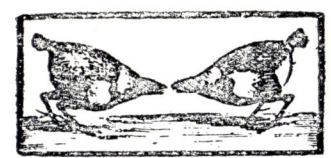

THE

GENTLEMEN's SUBSCRIPTION MAINS,

At Mr Loftus's Pit, Bigg-Market, Newcastle,

On Thursday, February 9th, 1809,—50l.			Friday,—50l.			Saturday,—100l.		
16 MR Hunter, red	3 10 0	Walton	13 MR Maddison, red	4 0 0	Welsh	10 MR Ridley, red		
2 Mr Story, red	3 10 0	Davidson	10 Mr Ridley, red			span.	4 4 0	Davidson
			dun	4 0 0	Davidson	6 Mr Dodd, dun	4 4 0	Walton
4 Mr Watson, red stag	3 10 0	Walton	8 Mr Wastell, bir.	4 0 0	Petree	3 Mr Watson, bir.	4 4 0	Walton
12 Mr Maddison, red dun	3 10 0	Welsh	14 Mr Taylor, red	4 0 0	Walton	2 Mr Milburn, yel.	4 4 0	Dubmore
13 Mr Taylor, red	3 10 0	Walton	15 Mr J. Watson, red	4 0 0	Walton	9 Mr Hudson, yel.	4 4 0	Walton
1 Mr Milburn, bir. pile	3 10 0	Dubmore	9 Mr Clark, red dun	4 0 0	Scott	4 Mr Mellish, bir. pile	4 4 0	Davidson
7 Mr Heslop, yel. span.	3 10 0	Lockey	11 Mr Hudson, black	4 0 0	Walton	13 Mr Maddison, yel.	4 4 0	Welsh
8 Mr Ridley, red span.	3 10 0	Davidson	1 Mr Baker, red	4 0 0	Dubmore	14 Mr Taylor, red	4 4 0	Walton
10 Mr Hudson, red	3 10 0	Walton	6 Mr Dodd, red dun	4 0 0	Walton	16 Mr Hunter, yel.	4 4 0	Walton
14 Mr Clark, bir. dun stag	3 10 0	Scott	5 Mr Mellish, red dun	3 15 3	Davidson	8 Mr Wastell, yel.	4 4 0	Petree
6 Mr Dodd, gin dun	3 10 0	Walton	3 Mr Milburn, bir pile	3 15 2	Dubmore	15 Mr J. Watson, red	4 4 0	Walton
9 Mr Wastell, red span.	3 10 0	Petree	12 Mr Johnson, red	3 15 2	Davidson	11 Mr Clark, bir. dun	4 4 0	Scott.
15 Mr J. Watson, red	3 10 0	Walton	2 Mr Story, red	3 15 0	Davidson	12 Mr Johnson, bir. pile	4 3 0	Davidson
11 Mr Johnson, red	3 10 0	Davidson	16 Mr Hunter, red dun	3 15 0	Walton	5 Mr Baker, bir. dun	4 3 0	Dubmore
3 Mr Baker, red	3 10 0	Dubmore	7 Mr Heslop, red	3 14 2	Lockey	1 Mr Story, red	4 3 0	Davidson
5 Mr Mellish, red	3 10 0	Davidson	4 Mr Watson, red	3 14 0	Walton	7 Mr Heslop, red	4 2 0	Lockey

To begin precisely at Eleven o'Clock each Day.

S. Hodgson, Printer, Newcastle.

COCK-FIGHTING

The barbarous sport of cock-fighting was once very popular in the north of England. As early as 1712 we have an advert for cock-fighting in Newcastle at the Crown outside Westgate. The advert below is from the *Chronicle* of December 1, 1770. The same paper contained six similar adverts and the total prize money was £720 (equivalent to £60,000 today!). The "sport" was patronised by the landed gentry. In 1790 a main was fought at Hexham between the Duke of Northumberland and Mr. Fenwick; in the same year at Alnwick the contestants were the Duke of Northumberland and Charles Grey versus Mr. Fenwick. Heavisides, the Stockton historian says:— "In the beginning of the present century (19th), when I resided at Darlington, there were two cock-pits at that place, one at the hole-in-the-Wall Inn, and the other at the Talbot, then the head hotel. The latter pit was very commodious, with tiers of seats all round, which used to be well attended by Sir Harry Vane, Lord Baynton, and other sporting gentlemen. The meetings at these pits were generally held for four days; three days for battles at £10 each, and the fourth day for a battle royal or Welsh main for £100. During these four days about one hundred and thirty noble birds were murdered, amidst the horrid oaths and imprecations of those who were called gentlemen. It is well the legislature put a stop to a practice so cruel and revolting."

Almost all the large inns of Newcastle had cock-pits. Most of the cocks were bred by pitmen and were brought into town well before the fights so they could be fed up to tip-top condition. When they fought they usually wore silver spurs.

The woodcut showing a country cock-fight is by Thomas Bewick and was one of his famous tailpieces.

TO be Fought for, at Mr. Mordue's New Pit in the Flesh Market, on Monday, the 31st of December, FIFTY POUNDS, by Cocks and Stags, 3lbs, 14oz.

On Tuesday, the 1st of January, ONE HUNDRED POUNDS, by Cocks and Stags, 4lb. 2oz.

On Wednesday, the 2nd, by Cocks, Stags, and Blenkards, 4lb. 2oz.

To weigh the Saturday before, between Ten and Twelve o'clock, and fight with fair Silver Spurs. The Stags for the Monday to be allowed one ounce; Tuesday, the Stags to be allowed one ounce and a half; and on Wednesday, the Stags to be allowed one ounce, and Blenkards one ounce and a half.

N.B.—Whereas, there have been many complaints made by the Gentlemen of the Sod in regard to their Cocks fighting with Candle Light, to prevent which for the future Mr. Mordue is determined to have a pair of Cocks upon the Sod precisely at Ten o'clock each Day.

5

A Bewick Tailpiece

Wylam Hopping.

MONDAY, July 28th. 1828.

1 A Donkey Race, for Half a Guinea
2 A Donkey Race, for 5s. *The last Ass to win*
   EACH JOCKEY TO RIDE HIS NEIGHBOUR'S ASS.
3 A Foot Race, for Half a Sovereign---Heats
4 A Foot Race, for 5s.
5 A Foot Race, for 2s. 6d. by Boys
6 A Soaped Pig Chase
7 To Grin for Tobacco
8 To Smoke for Tobacco
9 To Dive for Shillings in a Tub of Water
10 To Ferret for Half-Crowns in a Meal Tub
11 Race in Sacks, for a Crown
12 To eat Hot Hasty-Pudding, lifted by the
   Fingers, 2s. 6d.
13 For the best Hornpipe, 5s.
14 For the best Song, 2s. 6d.
15 For the best Whistler, 2s. 6d.
16 A Game Cock to be Hunted
17 A Pair of Gloves to Leap for
18 For him who can Eat 3 Penny Rolls the
   soonest, 2s. 6d.
   ☞ MANY OTHER PRIZES.

Sports to begin precisely at Three o'Clock.

Marshall, Printer, Newcastle.

THE NEWCASTLE RACE CUP.

CORVAN'S
THREE NEW SONGS !
Trip to Marsden Rock.
Maw Stepmother; and
He wad be a Noodle.
ALSO J. P. ROBSON'S
Landing o' the Frenchers
Cod Liver Oil; and
Horrid War i' Sangyet.

Published by W. Stewart, Head of the Side, Newcastle.

THE ROYAL

COMMERCIAL & FAMILY HOTEL,
NORTH BRIDGE STREET,
(CLOSE TO THE MONK WEARMOUTH STATION),
SUNDERLAND.

WILLIAM RICHARDSON begs to inform Commercial Gentlemen, his Friends, and the Public, that they will find the above Establishment conveniently situated, and hopes, by strict personal attention and moderate charges, to merit a share of their patronage.

GOOD STABLING AND LOCK-UP COACH HOUSE.
A SUPERIOR BILLIARD TABLE.
WINES & SPIRITS OF THE BEST DESCRIPTION.

INTERIOR OF THE GAOL, NEWCASTLE (1826). From the Entrance Tower.

PRISONS—OLD AND NEW

Over 100 years ago, in 1823 to be precise, a loud explosion was heard close by where the Co-operative Stores now stand. It was workmen blowing up the Newgate, the strongest and one of the oldest of mediaeval Newcastle's gates. With the end of Newgate went the old common goal of the town. From 1399, when Newcastle was made a county of itself, and took custody of its own prisoners, down to 1820 Newgate was the home of countless debtors and felons, many of whom spent their last days there, before being led out of the town's precincts up the Gallowgate (hence the name) and on to the Town Moor for execution.

Although in those days no real police force existed and so malefactors more easily escaped justice, nevertheless the laws were so severe that the goals were always full. Since the penalty for robbery was usually death hangings were a frequent occurrence. Those who failed to pay their debts found it even more difficult to do so by being put in Newgate till their debts were paid. A few were lucky enough on special occasions to have their debts paid by public subscription. Once in prison however they were allowed certain liberties and at Newgate they could walk in a small garden at the back as far as the Lork Burn which ran near the present Darn Crook. This area was called Execution Dock, since the debtors were in prison till the execution of their sentence i.e. till their debt was paid. Occasionally at times of public rejoicing subscriptions raised to pay the debts of a few of Newgate's prisoners. From Execution Dock the debtors could enjoy the sight of the town pillory which lay a little further down Newgate Street.

What happened to the prisoners once in goal was nobody's business. In fact Newgate was only heated at the time of Sir William Blackett, who gave the prisoners a regular ration of coal from his mines at Cambo. However, though conditions were bad, there was one consolation — it was easier to escape and the annals of Newgate are full of successful and attempted escapes. We read of the fat prisoner who while escaping got stuck in the chimney and of another who almost made a hole right through the thick walls to safety.

The most remarkable escape however took place in 1736. One of the prison's turnkeys named Thomas Tate turned thief and found himself lodged in Newgate as a prisoner. Although chained to the wall he made an ingenious escape and then had the nerve to return and rob the keeper's house, enter the room he had occupied as a turnkey and having donned his Sunday best left the prison. On rearrest he once again escaped till at last he was sent to the Plantations.

But Newgate went, in spite of a big agitation in the town to preserve this historic gate. It ceased to be the jail because the judges at the Assize had declared it "out of repair, inconvenient, insufficient and insecure."

While a new prison was in construction the debtors were placed in the great hall of the castle which we are told was "lofty, airy, and comfortable." As we can see today it was certainly lofty and airy but whether comfortable is a matter for question.

During the period when Newgate was in use the Castle was still used as the county prison. One of our worthy historians the Rev. Brand tells us: "Its great coolness makes it very fit for being a beer cellar throughout the year and a prison for felons during the assizes." When Howard the prison reformer visited it in the 18th century he found the conditions disgusting. He described the prisoners "both men and women," as being "confined together 7 or 8 nights, in a dirty, damp dungeon, six steps in the old Castle, which, having no roof, in a wet season the water is some inches deep. The felons are chained to rings in the walls."

When Howard visited Newgate he was very favourably impressed. He describes it as follows:—

"In this Newgate, which is the gate at the upper end of the town, all the rooms except the condemned room are upstairs, and airy: I always found them remarkably clean, strewed with sand, etc. The corporation allow both

STOCKS IN JARROW CHURCHYARD.

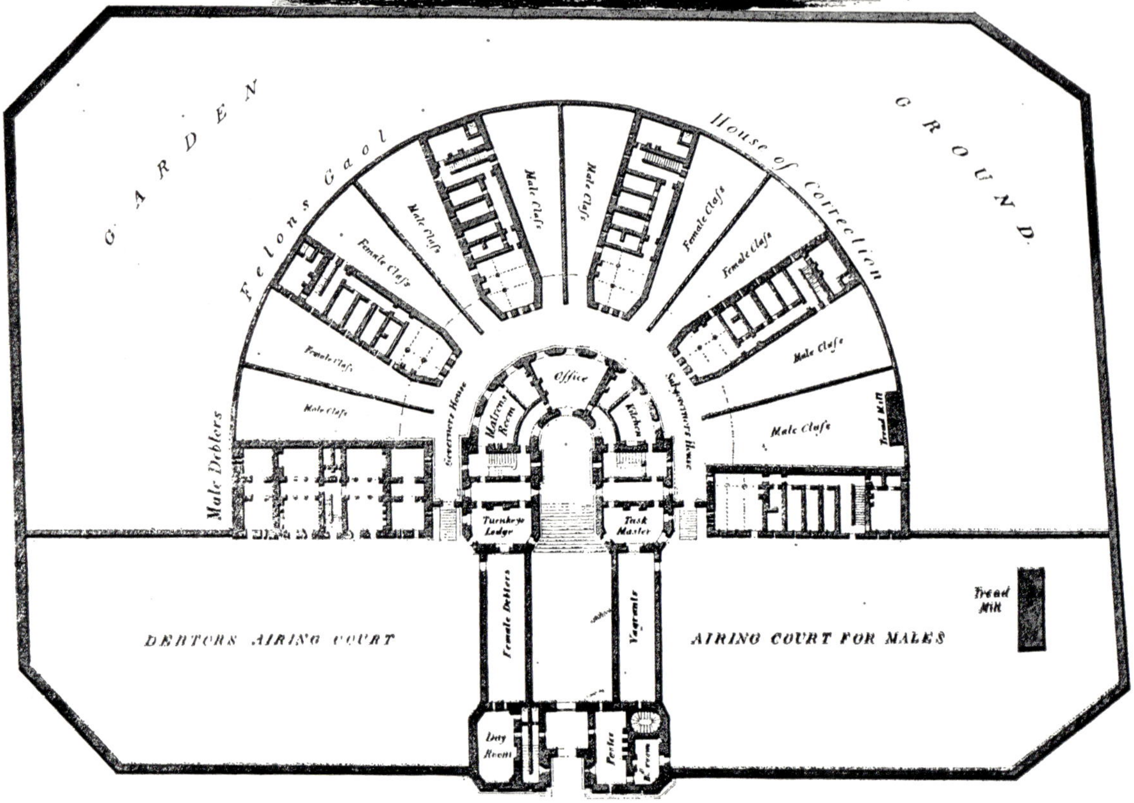

PLAN OF THE NEW PRISONS IN NEWCASTLE.

debtors and felons firing and candles in plenty: and every prisoner has a chaff bed, two blankets, and a coverlet: debtors and felons are thus accomodated in few other prisons in England. They also allow brooms, mops, and all such necessaries. The sums generously allowed for those articles, amount to £40 12s. 8d. per annum."

At this time and for many years afterwards the prisoners in the Castle were on Assize Sunday shown to the populace like wild beasts, price 6d admission.

Ralph Gardiner, the South Shields brewer, who in the 17th century made such a brave stand for the rights of his native town against the Newcastle Corporation was confined there. As he had been imprisoned for brewing beer in Shields in defiance of the Newcastle monopoly he was particularly displeased because he was "constrained to drink the gaoler's beer, not fit for mens' bodies."

The drawing by Paul Brown (1937) shows the remains of a prison under Elvet Bridge at the left of the city end of the bridge It was in a cell here that Jemmy Allan the famous piper died in 1809.

Entrance to prison below Elvet Bridge

Even the Newgate and the Castle were not adequate in olden times and we find other places being used. Petty offenders accused of being drunk and disorderly, or improper and lewd conduct were confined in the tower on the old Tyne Bridge. Like the Castle this prison seems to have been connected with the brewing business. For we read that Harry Wallis, a master shipwright, for being drunk and abusing the Puritan Alderman Barnes was confined there. In his cell he found a quantity of malt which he threw out of the window with a shovel into the Tyne singing the following ditty:—

> "O base malt,
> Thou didst the fault,
> And into Tyne thou shalt."

Newcastle also had its Borstal for unruly apprentices who were sent there by their masters' guilds. The guild rules for apprentices were so strict that we can understand the goaler at the Westgate where they were confined fully earning his salary of 40s. per year.

One of the guilds forbade its apprentices to dance or use musick in the streets. Their apparel to be under 103s. or if fustian under 3s. No velvet or lace; no silk garters. "Neither shall they wear their hair long, nor locks at their ears like ruffians."

During the days of the Civil War trouble with the apprentices seems to have been at its height and in 1648 seventeen apprentices were locked up in Westgate, perhaps because their garb offended their masters. But on a dark and stormy night they escaped by a rope through the privy. Eventually the guilds found the apprentices so much trouble that they put the responsibility on the individual master craftsmen. We read: "the merchants soon grew tired of the struggle, and decided that considering the continual trouble their fellowship hath had at every court since holden, to bring them to conformity, it is ordered that every man shall regulate his own apprentice, failing to do which, the master was to be fined three pounds for each offence without forgiveness"

Whether this solved the problem we don't know, but very much doubt.

Newcastle, as everyone knows also had its royal prisoner, Charles I. His prison was the finest house in the town near where Andrson Place afterwards stood.

With the end of the Newgate the prison planners got busy and the Town Mayor Archibold Reed with the enthusiastic support of a well known local architect proposed a grandiose scheme for a penitentiary on the site of the Castle with castellated buildings and lofty walls to blend with the Keep which was to be the centre of the whole ensemble And so we would have had the castle which had defended early Newcastle becoming once again a prison for its less fortunate inhabitants and the whole scheme of such a grandiose design as would have made us a mockery everywhere.

However such a foolish plan was not to be, and in 1823 a new prison was opened in Carliol Street with ringing of church bells, firing of cannon, military parades, silver trowels, and all the usual pageantry which to us would appear rather inappropriate in the opening of a modern prison.

In still earlier days religious offences were punished by the Bishop of Durham. Penances were often imposed for moral and ecclesiastical offences and it was no uncommon sight to see some poor offender standing shivering outside St. Nicholas clad only in a linen gown, calling out his offence and latter being whipped by the priest.

KNOCKING-UP SLATE

The *slate* shown on this drawing was once common in Durham mining villages It is a "knocking-up" slate. In the days before alarm clocks getting up for the early shift was a problem. A "knocker-up" was employed to go round the village and the time was chalked on the slate for waking. He carried a pole and where the house was of two storeys he tapped on the window above where the miner slept.

The inscription on the cup reads:
Presented to Mr. Geo Dunn the 2?th Nov. 1805 ... tribute of respect and Gratitude by 50 KEELMEN who were imprest into the LAPWING Capt. A. Skene at SHIELDS in May 1803 and taken to the NORE where by his exertion they were discharged he also obtained for them £65/... PRIZE Money for the Capture of a DUTCH EAST INDIAMAN whilst serving on board the LAPWING

THE KEELMAN'S CUP

This silver cup in the Laing Art Gallery is an interesting piece of Tyneside social history.

During the Napoleonic Wars there was a great demand for men for the Navy The supply of men was provided by the press-gangs which were active on Tyneside because so many suitable men resided here In March 1803 Captain Mackenzie was posted to Tyneside to obtain men for the Navy but he found his work difficult Apart from the Corporation of Newcastle, one of whose members loaned him a tender he received little support locally. On the 19th of April a foray was made into Sunderland but without success Mackenzie wrote:—

Lieutenant Bounton has this instant come away to inform me, that he durst not attempt to impress at that place last night, as Mobs of hundreds of Seamen, Soldiers and Women, got round the Rendezvous and threatened the lives of himself and People, whether they acted or not.

The local magistrate and garrison commander refused to help. The same day Lieutenant Mitchell took a gang into South Shields He was: *attacked by a Multitude of Pilots and Women who threw a quantity of Stones and Brickbatts at him, they likewise threatened to hew him down with their spades, which are very dangerous weapons, they being round and quite sharp, with shanks of about six feet in length, and likewise threatened to Murder him if ever he came back.*

Once again the local magistrates refused to help: they were "away from home". The Admiralty then ordered him to seize workers who were normally exempt such as keelmen. His first attempt at South Shields on April 28th failed and one local J.P. actively opposed the press-gang. But on May 10th he was successful in seizing 53 keelmen at Shields. He reported to the Admiralty:

There are a vast body of fine men in the Keels who were protected by their Lordships. Captain Skene and myself determined to take as many of the young ones as we could this morning, leaving all Skippers.

The immediate result was a strike by all the keelmen on Tyneside who had the tacit support of the coalowners. A leading figure in the coal trade George Dunn went to London to negotiate with the Admiralty for their release. He obtained such an order but when he reached the Nore (the naval base at the mouth of the Thames) just as the man of war the *Lapwing* arrived with the keelmen from the Tyne, the order was countermanded.

Returning to London Dunn obtained the help of two local M.P.'s Matthew Ridley and George Burden and eventually had the men freed. One of the conditions was that in future the keelmen would have to provide substitutes on a one-in-ten basis. It was a Pyrrhic victory and it has been suggested that the whole affair was planned by the Navy in order to obtain some such concession. On returning to Tyneside the keelmen presented the cup to George Dunn and a few days later Captain Mackenzie "broke his leg" and was replaced by William Charlton.

The cup has no marks on it but was almost certainly made by one of the local silversmiths.

Sir Charles Trevelyan speaking at the City Hall

THEY FOUGHT IN SPAIN

The north of England has always supported people fighting for freedom in their own countries. When Garibaldi visited the Tyne in 1854 he was presented with a sword and telescope purchased by a penny subscription. The presentation was made by a group of people following a large public meeting, including Jospeh Cowan and prominent Chartists and radicals. The sword and telescope were engraved with the following words — "Presented to General Garibaldi by the people of Tyneside, friends of European Freedom, Newcastle-on-Tyne, April, 1854".

When the War of Intervention against the young Soviet Republic took place after the 1st World War the trade union movement on Tyneside played a great part in forcing Churchill to withdraw the British troops from Archangel in Northern Russia.

When the struggle against fascism broke out in Spain in 1936 and the International Brigade was formed to assist the Spanish people more than one hundred men from Northumberland and Durham volunteered to fight for Spanish democracy. Twenty-four laid down their lives. Our illustrations show the packed memorial meeting held in their honour in January 1939 in the City Hall, Newcastle. The speaker is Sir Charles Trevelyan.

Badge of the International Brigades

Below is title page of the paper of the 15th Brigade to which the British Battalion belonged.

Numéro 25 - 14 Avril 1937 - VI Anniversaire de la République Espagnole

JOURNAL DE LA 15ème BRIGADE INTERNATIONALE

12

MEMORIAL MEETING
IN HONOUR

of the NORTH EAST MEN of the BRITISH BATTALION who laid down their Lives in Spain.

Coun. BOB ELLIOTT.

IN THE

CITY HALL

NEWCASTLE upon TYNE

SUNDAY, 15th. JANUARY, 1939.

at 7.30 p.m.   Doors open at 7 p.m.

CLIFF LAWTHER.

Speakers—

Sir CHARLES TREVELYAN,

WILL LAWTHER, (M.F.G.B.)

HAMILTON FYFE,

F. M. GRAHAM, (British Battalion)

JOHN GOSS of London, will Sing.

WILF JOBLING.

Supported by :—

Miss ELLEN WILKINSON, M.P.	DAVID ADAMS, M.P.	WILLIAM WHITELY, M.P.
J. CHUTER EDE, M.P.	J. J. LAWSON, M.P.	SAM WATSON, Agent D.M.A.

LYALL WILKES, Prospective Labour Candidate, Central Division, Newcastle.

ARTHUR BLENKINSOP, Prospective Labour Candidate, East Division, Newcastle.

JAMES BOWMAN, Sec., N.M.A.   Coun. WM. ALLAN.   Miss ENID ATKINSON.

WILLIAM HEPPLE, (A. E. U.)

International Brigaders entering the City Hall

"Bedstead" tram at Pier Head, South Shields, 1887   South Tyneside Public Libraries and Museum

Many of the sports and pastimes we know today were practiced 100 years ago. However the most popular sport in the 19th century — professional rowing — has disappeared from the Tyne. Foot racing for money, once exceedingly common, has now virtually ceased. The brutal game of prizefighting has gone but its modern counterpart is on the decline. in the north east. Large money prizes in running and rowing were competed for last century but the gigantic commercialism of "sport" today was unknown.

South Tyneside Public Libraries and Museums

15

Drawn and Engraved by W. Martin the Natural Philosopher Northumberland

PRIZEFIGHTING AT BLYTH

Prizefighting was once a popular but illegal sport. The engraving by William Martin recalls a famous fight which took place at Middleton near Blyth The contestants were the famous negro fighter, Young Molyneaux, and a local man called Will Renwick The prize money was £25 and the fight took place on October 31st, 1837 "Will Renwick, a blacksmith from Winlaton, was widely known as a bare-fisted fighter and took part in numerous battles at Hedley Moor, on the Northumberland and Durham border, this spot being favoured because it was easy for the men to nip over the border into the next county if there was any interference from the law!"

At Middleton an attempt was made to stop the fight by Mr Thomas Anderson, J.P. of Little Harle Tower. The Anderson family had for many years lived at the famous Anderson House in Newcastle and it was only four years earlier that Thomas had sold his Newcastle home to Richard Grainger and moved to Little Harle His attempt to stop the fight seems to have failed.

It was a bloody struggle lasting for one and a half hours consisting of 87 rounds, forty of which were fought in darkness. Young Malyneaux was the victor after several butts with his head had knocked out young Renwick.

(Based on an article by Joan Gale in the Blyth News of November 6th, 1969).

The artist William Martin was one of the "mad" Martins. His brother John Martin was the celebrated Victorian painter whose dramatic canvasses drew crowds when exhibited. After a period when his work was forgotten he has now come back into favour and is acknowledged as one of the great painters of the North. William's other brother, Jonathan, achieved fame by setting fire to York Minster. He ended his life in the Bethlehem Hospital for Lunatics in 1838.

William Martin was certainly unbalanced but was also a man of great talent. In 1821 he published his best known work — *A New System of Natural Philosophy* — which was a refutation of Sir Isaac Newton's theory. He was an inventor of great originality. The lack of recognition which his inventions and writings received undoubtedly affected his mind. He became an eccentric and was well known in Newcastle where he paraded the streets wearing large medals which he had designed and presented to himself. He did engraving on copper and steel and published numerous pamphlets mainly about his inventtions and philosophical ideas.

CLOG DANCING

Writing of his boyish impressions of Newcastle in 1881 George Fothergill refers to the fact that the "steel-workers' clogs were not inaudible to us as they rattled over the large cobbles in Castle Garth and down the steep Castle Stairs." In 1902 he once again had to descend the steps and noticed that clogs were still "going strong" (though not *so* strong as twenty years ago) as evidenced by the fact that there were no less than four clog-shops situated on the "Castle Stairs" Industrial clogs have now disappeared in Northumberland and Durham. Clog dancing, however, still survives and is now staging a come back. The origins of clog-dancing are obscure but it was almost entirely centred on the mining villages where competitions were common before the second World War Charlie Chaplin made his debut on the stage as a clog dancer. He was one of the famous troupe called the "8 Lancashire Lads" and from 1897 to 1900 he toured most of the northern music halls.

The industrial clog was usually protected by iron plates called *coakers* but those used for dancing had the irons removed. and were a flat type often ornately decorated. The clog dancer's dress shows its mining origin. These were velvet kneebreeches like miners' working *hoggers*, a shirt, a velvet waistcoat (compare the dress of the keelmen) and a bright sash tied round the waist.

An old Clog sign — Down the Castle Stairs Newcastle on Tyne

DURHAM MINERS' ASSOCIATION

On November 20th, 1869 a group of miners met in a room of the Market Hotel, Durham, to form a miners' trade union. The building still stands and can be seen in our drawing Although no official records of the meeting have survived there was a detailed report in the *Durham Chronicle*. Here is a selection of their resolutions:—

"That the following be appointed Trustees — Alan Murray, W. Clarke, Isaac Parks, W. Patterson, R. Carr, W. Wilson, John Armstrong and T. Noble . . . that each delegate have one vote . . . that Mr. John Richardson be Agent and Secretary and be paid 32s. per week and allowed third-class railway fare when on the business of the association when such business calls him more than

four miles from his residence, the delegates to decide his place of residence . . . that the miners of the County of Durham have their attention called to the objects contemplated by the Association by hand-bills and that 500 be printed . . . that the agent go into the Crook and Spennymoor districts and explain the advantages of the Society . . ."

The following year William Crawford was appointed agent and spent the rest of his life in building the Durham Miners' Association.

17

A woodcut from Bewick's workshop

In our local papers and books of the last century there are many delightful engravings of the shops to be found in our towns and villages. They are in startling contrast to the monotonous and ugly shops built by the "multiples" of today. Each shop had a character of its own and the shop fronts (before the invention of plastic) were the work of craftsmen. A number of them have survived but they are definitely an endangered species. They stand out in defiance of the "planners" and "architects" of today and their enemies are steadily destroying them. One dreadful example of official vandalism has just occurred in Hexham. The beautiful chemist shop of Gibson's, whose interior and exterior have survived for over a century, was gutted last year. Its exterior has received a temporary reprieve but its days are probably numbered. There were no multiples in those days. The names of many of their owners were known throughout the area. They were genuine family concerns with a reputation for service. They have almost entirely disappeared. The Eldon Square KOMPLEX and our city motorway murdered dozens of them. A few survive in name only. They are owned by large foreign and southern combines. Fenwick's is probably the only large

South Tyneside Public Libraries and Museums

family shop still surviving today in Newcastle. In the smaller market towns the process has not yet been carried so far.

18

NEWCASTLE UPON TYNE.

AT a General Meeting of the Proprietors of the Assembly-Rooms, held the 28th of February 1786,

RESOLVED UNANIMOUSLY, That a Master of the Ceremonies shall be appointed, to conduct the public Amusements in these Rooms.

That he shall continue in Office till removed by a Majority at a General Meeting of the Proprietors.

That his Commands respecting the Ceremonies shall be implicitly obeyed by all Ladies and Gentlemen attending these Amusements; and if any shall act contrary to his Orders, the Person so offending shall thereafter be refused Admittance into these Rooms, until such Submission and Atonement shall be made as the Committee for the Time being shall direct.

That the Master of the Ceremonies shall observe such Orders and Regulations as shall be made by the Committee for the Time being; but if he shall at any Time be dissatisfied with such Orders and Regulations, he may direct the Secretary to call a General Meeting of the Proprietors to adjust and settle the same.

That if any Person shall be dissatisfied with the Conduct of the Master of the Ceremonies, Complaint may be made to the Committee for the Time being, who shall hear the same, and grant such Redress as they shall think fit.

ORDERS and REGULATIONS of the COMMITTEE
pursuant to the above RESOLUTIONS.

Every Gentleman intending to dance Country Dances shall, before he enters the Rooms, draw a Number, which shall determine his Place in the Country Dances for the Night; but if he shall neglect to take his Place when the Country Dances begin, he shall, if he dances afterwards, stand at the Bottom of the last Set.

Ladies entitled to Precedency shall take Place accordingly, in Minuets and Country Dances; every other Lady to dance Minuets in the Order in which she shall happen to sit.

The Country Dances to consist of Sets, not exceeding Fifteen Couples each Set; and if there shall be more Sets than can conveniently dance at the same Time, the first and other Sets, in the Order they stand, after having danced one Dance, shall retire, and the other Sets which have not danced shall stand up; and so on alternately.

The Couple in each Set who shall have led down a Dance shall stand last Couple of that Set the next Dance.

The Dances shall be called by the Couples to lead off in each Set progressively; the first Set to call the first Dance, the second Set the second Dance, and so on.

No Couple shall sit down until the whole Set shall have danced to the Bottom, except in Case of Illness, under which Circumstance it is expected such Couple will not dance again that Night.

Minuets shall always commence at Eight o'Clock, Tea be prepared at the Time the Master of the Ceremonies shall appoint, and the Dancing shall cease at One o'Clock.

Strangers must be introduced to the Master of the Ceremonies, that proper Attention may be paid to them.

The Members of the Committee will assist the Master of the Ceremonies in procuring Gentlemen to dance Minuets, that his Attention may not be diverted from the Ladies.

RICHARD FISHER, Secretary.

THE ASSEMBLY ROOMS

Built in 1776 the Assembly Rooms has recently celebrated the 200th anniversary of its foundation. It is one of the finest buildings in Newcastle and has played an important part in the social life of the city. However sixty years before, the old Assembly Rooms stood on the opposite side of the street in a house *"formally belonging to Sir William Creagh"*. Here dances and masquerades were held until about 1736 when new rooms were built in the Groat Market. Here the wealthy people of Newcastle held their meetings for 40 years until the present building was erected.

The new Assembly Rooms cost £6,000. There were 129 shareholders holding 234 shares of £25 each and the Corporation donated £200.

William Newton's building, in the Adam style, was an ornament to the city. The Great Ball Room, with its fine plasterwork and magnificent chandeliers is the gem of the building. A brochure tells us that *"the seven gorgeous chandeliers of scintillating crystal depending from the ceiling are superb in their brilliance"*. The centre chandelier, a massive gem, is reputed to have cost 600 guineas, and it is interesting to note that these chandeliers have now been used for three methods of lighting, by candle, gas, and electricity.

During the 200 years of its history many important events have taken place in the Assembly Rooms. In 1827 a grand ball was given when the Duke of Wellington visited the city. We are told that 691 of the gentry of the North attended and the "august" gathering started to dance with the tune of the Keel Row, a rather innappropriate melody. The opening of the Newcastle and Darlington Railway was celebrated with George Hudson, the *Railway King*, in the chair.

When it was reopened shortly after the First World War an advertising brochure tells us "the traditions of the building lend a glamour and dignity to all gatherings within its walls, for from time to time the elegant Rooms have been graced by eminent Northumbrians. Their sons and daughters have once more the privilege within these handsome precincts of recapturing the spirit of the past and rekindling memories hallowed by treasured associations."

ON STRIKE

Our picture is from the *Daily Graphic* of 1892 and shows Durham miners outside the 'B' pit at Hebburn. The great strike of 1892 was against a wage cut, and in the course of it the owners doubled the size of the cut they were demanding. The men refused to settle. They held out for 3 months and went back united, and though they had to accept a cut it was not of the full amount claimed.

HEXHAM SANITATION

Young man! if you propose to yourself to commence life as a sanitary reformer be prepared to encounter contumely, bigotry, prejudice, and narrow minded selfishness in one direction, ignorance and a misapprehension of your motives on the other. It is hard dreary up hill toil is sanitary reform.

We have been disappointed in our report from Hexham, but we learn that the election of the first Board of Health for the Hexham district took place on the Monday after New Year's day, with the following results.

Nine gentlemen, well known as Sanitary Reformers, were defeated by nine others, pledged to "keep down the rates", and allow matters to go on in what is called "the good old way". It was boasted by the opposition that they would poll 5 to 1, but the issue showed the relative strength of parties to be 3 to 2. When it is considered that, two years ago, the question of Public Health was scarcely spoken of, and its supporters did not number above a dozen, while now not less than 400 have by their votes declared their adherence to the cause of Sanitary Reform, the result, in one sense, so far from being considered a defeat, will be held as furnishing matter for congratulation. There is no place in the North of England needs a thorough cleansing more than Hexham. Its streets are almost without a sewer; foul privies, ashpits and cesspools abound; and water is supplied impure in quality and deficient in quantity, and only by pants or wells; for house service is at present impossible. This want of even a pretence of sanitary arrangement produces its inevitable result in the high average mortality of the town. For the last seven years the death rate has been 29 in 1,000; but during the last twelve months it has risen to 34, exclusive of the deaths from cholera. This mortality, exceeding that of Liverpool or Glasgow, and occurring near districts celebrated for their healthiness, justifies the conclusion that the town of Hexham must be seriously defective in many regulations necessary for a healthy and comfortable existence.

From the Northern Tibune. 1864

WILLIAM DAVISON

The great Alnwick printer William Davison (1781-1858), was an outstanding north country printer who during the nineteenth century published from his press numerous books and pamphlets of great merit. He has been described as "the most brilliant ornamental printer of his time".

He commenced business as a pharmacist, which he combined with the sale of stationery and printing. His printing career started in partnership with John Catnach, a printer of quality who employed Thomas Bewick to engrave many of his blocks.

Davison became famous for his chapbooks which are now considered to be some of the finest ever published. In 1854 Davison started the first Alnwick newspaper — the *Alnwick Mercury* — which when he died had a circulation of 2,600, a remarkable sale for a small provincial newspaper. In 1884 the *Mercury* was amalgamated with the *Alnwick County Gazette* and still continues publication as the weekly *Northumbrian Gazette*.

LETTERPRESS AND COPPERPLATE PRINTING NEATLY EXECUTED

ORDERS AND ADVERTISEMENTS RECEIVED FOR ALL THE LONDON AND PROVINCIAL NEWSPAPERS.

TEA, COFFEE, AND TOBACCO PAPERS, WITH ORNAMENTAL LABELS, PRINTED AT A CHEAP RATE.

NEW BOOKS, MAGAZINES, REVIEWS, AND ALL PERIODICAL PUBLICATIONS REGULARLY ORDERED FROM LONDON.

W. DAVISON,
BOOKSELLER, STATIONER, PRINTER, &c.
NO. 22, BONDGATE STREET, ALNWICK,
SELLS THE FOLLOWING ARTICLES, WHOLESALE AND RETAIL, ON THE LOWEST TERMS:—

Account Books
Albums in elegant Bindings
Almanacks
Alphabets and Primers for Children
Arithmetics and other School Books
Ass-Skin and other Memorandum Books
Ass-Skin prepared
Atlasses
Auction Sheets
Backgammon Tables
Barrie's and other Class Books for Schools
Bibles, Testaments, Prayer Books, &c. remarkably cheap
Bill Books
Black-Bordered Paper
Black-Lead Pencils
Black Lines
Blank Cards
Blotting Cases and Paper
Bonnet Boards
Books, new and second-hand, an extensive assortment on all subjects, at very reduced Prices
Brief Paper
Bristol Drawing Boards
Brushes, Hair, Nail, &c.
Camel Hair and other Pencils
Camera Lucida
Candle Ornaments
Card Boards
Cards, plain, gilt-edged, mourning, and tinted
Cards, Playing, white or fancy back, coloured, &c.
Catechisms of all kinds
Cartridge Papers, all sizes, for drawing and general use
Cedar Pencil Sticks
Chalk Pencils
Children's Books in great variety
Chinese Paper & Ornaments
Churches in the Diocese of Durham, Views of
Chip Boxes

Ciphering Books
Coloured Inks
Coloured Papers, all kinds
Colours for Children
Colours, superfine, in Boxes or Cakes
Compasses, Scales, & Mathematical Instruments
Cookery Books
Copy Books and Copy Lines
Copying Paper for Letter Books, &c.
Day Books, Ledgers, &c.
Dictionaries, Grammars, &c.
Drawing Boards, white and tinted
Drawing Books
Drawing Papers, all sizes, from Demy to Antiquarian
Drawing Pencils
Dutch Metal
Envelopes, all sizes, in packets and cases
Filtering Paper
Folders, Ivory and Bone
Forril, White, Green, &c.
French Tracing Paper
Gold and Silver Leaf
Gold-Beater's Skin
Gold Paper, Borders, and Ornaments
Hair for Violin Bows
Hutton's Arithmetic, enlarged and Improved. Also a complete Key to the Work
Highway Account and Rate Books
India Rubber, Bottle and Patent
Ink, Indian
Ink Powders, Red, Black, &c.
Inkstands
Ink, Writing, Black, Red, Blue, &c.
Initial Wafers
Ivory Folders
Japan Writing Ink
Ledgers and other Account Books at very low prices
Letter Clip, Patent, for securing Letters, Invoices, &c.

Letter Files
Letter Paper, embellished with beautiful engravings by Bewick and other Artists
Letter Writers
London Drawing Boards
Manganese Ink
Maps
Marble Papers
Marking Ink for Linen, Silk, &c.
Mathematical Instruments, in Sets, &c.
Memorandum Books of all sizes, plain, ruled, Ass-Skin, Metallic, &c.
Mill Boards
Morocco Paper
Musical Instruments
Music Paper and Music Books
Northumberland, Views of Castles and Gentlemen's Seats in
Note Papers, plain, gilt, black-bordered, &c. of all sizes and qualities
Ornamental Papers
Packing and Shop Papers of all kinds
Paper Hangings, great variety of patterns from 8d. to 24s. the piece
Parallel Rulers
Parchment
Pasteboards
Patent Medicines, all sorts
Pencils, Black-Lead, Crayon, Camel-Hair, Fitch, Swan-Quill, &c.
Pencils, Blacklead, Red, &c. and Pencil Points
Pen Holders
Pens at reduced Prices
Pens, Portable and Steel
Pink Saucers
Playing Cards
Pocket Books
Poonah Brushes
Poors' Rate Books
Portfolios

Post Paper, plain, gilt-edged, mourning, &c.
Pounce
Prayer Books, great variety
Pressings
Psalm and Hymn Books
Quills of superior quality
Razor Straps .
Reading Easy and Primers
Ready Reckoners
Rent Distress Forms
Rice Paper
Ruled Writing Papers for Accounts, &c.
Rulers, Ebony, Cedar, &c.
Ruling Pens
School Books of all kinds
Scrap Books
Sealing Wax, of all colours and qualities
Seals, Alphabet and Motto
Shining Sand
Silent Matches
Silver Leaf
Sketch Books
Slates and Slate Pencils
Song Books in great variety
Spelling Books, Mavor's, Markham's, Guy's, &c.
Sponge
Steel Pens and Holders
Tissue Paper, white and coloured
Toy Playing Cards
Tracing Papers
Tunbridge Boxes, Colours
Valentines and Valentine Books
Varnishing Brushes
Vellum Paper
Violin and Violoncello Strings, Bridges, and Pegs
Violins and Bows
Wafers, Motto & Alphabet
Wafers of all sizes and Wafer Seals
Walking Sticks
Washing Books
Water Colours in Cakes and Boxes
Writing Copies
Writing Paper of all kinds.

LIBRARIES REPAIRED, CATALOGUED, OR VALUED.
OLD BOOKS exchanged.

PRINTING & STEREOTYPING
done by contract.
HANDBILLS, CARDS, CIRCULARS, INVOICES, CATALOGUES, WINDOW BILLS, SHOP LABELS, REPORTS, PAMPHLETS, SERMONS, TRACTS, MATHEMATICAL WORKS, AND ALL KINDS OF BOOK PRINTING NEATLY AND CORRECTLY EXECUTED.

BOOKS ELEGANTLY AND SUBSTANTIALLY BOUND IN THE BEST MANNER.

LET US ALL BE UNHAPPY TOGETHER.

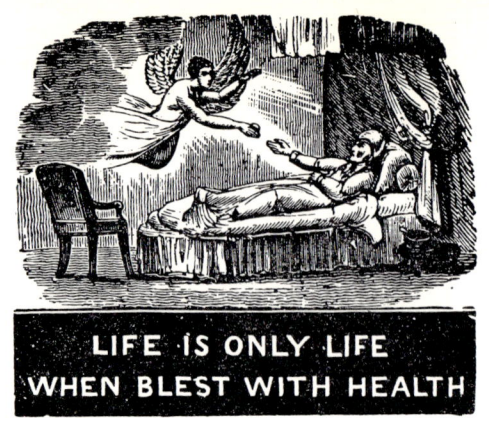

LIFE IS ONLY LIFE
WHEN BLEST WITH HEALTH

THE OLD MAIDS PETITION

Sweet Powder.

YAWNING IS CATCHING.

Humorous prints by W. Davison of Alnwick

Some adverts from Bewick's workshop

CHEAP TRAIN.

Wrestling Match

BETWEEN

IVISON, OF CARLISLE, AND

JAMESON, OF NEWCASTLE, AT

HAYDON BRIDGE

On TUESDAY, July 29, 1845.

The Public are respectfully informed, that the Directors of the Newcastle and Carlisle Railway Company have kindly consented to an application to convey Passengers FROM NEWCASTLE (and all Intermediate Stations) TO HAYDON BRIDGE and back, for

One Fare,

By the Train which leaves the Newcastle Station at 7 o'clock in the Morning of the above day---to return by the Trains in the Evening.

Newcastle, July 16, 1845.

Printed by W. DOUGLAS, Observer Office, High Street, Gateshead.

ROBERT SMITH SURTEES *1805-1864*

No British writer of merit has been so disregarded by his contemporaries and received such unjust treatment at the hands of literary critics and historians as Robert Surtees the realist sporting writing of early Victorian days. Locally also he is hardly known although he is one of the greatest of Northumbrian writers. Almost alone the *Cambridge History of English Literature* does Surtees justice. "Surtees is", writes Harold Child, "a comic writer of a broad and hearty humour and a deft and subtle touch. In the invention of comic character and speech, he comes second only to Dickens. Mr. Jorrocks, 'Facey' Romford, Lord Scamperdale and his friend Jack Spraggon, Mr. Sponge, Mr. Jawleyford of Jawleyford Court — these, with nearly every character that Surtees troubles to elaborate, are rich in humour; while the dialogue in these novels has a force and flavour comparable only with that in Dickens, or in some pieces of flourishing invective in Nashe or Greene. Surtees's comedy is, doubtless, like that of Dickens, mainly a comedy of 'humours' or personal oddities; and Surtees, it must be admitted, was careless about construction and about such necessary parts of a novel as did not interest him; but all the fun is rooted in human nature, and set out with abounding energy."

Surtees was born on May 17th, 1805, at The Riding, Northumberland but while he was still a child the family moved to Hamsterley Hall near Rowlands Gill. He was educated at Ovingham, attending the boarding school in the parsonage, the same place where Thomas Bewick had earlier received his education. Later he went to Durham Grammar School.

His first publication (apart from a legal treatise on Horses) was *Jorrocks's Jaunts and Jollities*, 1838, a collection of some of his best journalistic sketches taken from the "New Sporting Magazine".

Surtees had now settled down as the squire of Hamsterley Hall and after a brief political episode when he stood for Parliament at Gateshead, he lived the rest of his life as a country gentleman.

In 1843 Surtees published his most famous work, *Handley Cross*, which had appeared in serial form from 1836. It was a complete failure. The patrons of fox-hunting disliked the way in which Jorrocks, a mere city grocer, made fools of them and their conventions while the middle class at that time considered everything connected with foxhunting as sheer madness.

The book, like most of Surtees novels, was set in the north country and the characters were drawn from local people whom Surtees knew. The prototype of Jorrocks the Cockney grocer was a local tailor from Newcastle, while James Pigg is the first Novocastrian in English literature. Here is the famous passage where Jorrocks and Pigg met for the first time:—

"Vere d'ye come from?"

"Cannynewcassel," replied Pigg . . . "Ar's a native of Paradise (part of the Scotswood road area!!) aside Cannynewcassel — ye'll ken Cannynewcassel, nae doubt," observed he, running the words together.

"Carn't say as 'ow I do," replied Mr. Jorrocks thoughtfully, still eyeing the bird of Paradise. "Is it any way near Dundee"?

"Dundee! No — what should put that i' your head?" snapped Pigg.

"Wot should put that i' my 'ead!" retorted Mr. Jorrocks, boiling up. "Vy, it must be near somewhere!"

"Near somewhere!" now exclaimed Pigg, indignant at the slight thus put on his famous city. "Why, it's a great town of itsel' — ye surely ken Newcassel where arle the coals come frae?"

"You said Candied Newcassel," enunciated Mr. Jorrocks, slowly and emphatically — "You said Candied Newcassel," repeated he, "From which I naturally concluded it was near Dundee, where they make the candied confectionary. I get my marmeylad from there. I'm not such a hignorant hass," continued he, "As not to know where Newcastle is. I've been i' Scotland myself! Durham at least."

They then took a good long stare at each other, each thinking the other a 'rum un'.

Pigg's dialect of course, that of a real Geordie, is constantly made fun of by Surtees. In the trial scene of Handley Cross after suggesting that an interpreter was needed for Pigg the judge goes on; "First, you have James Pigg, the huntsman, who informs us in subterranean language — if, indeed, it can be called a language — that he said 'nout', which, I suppose, is meant to imply that he did not warrant the horse; the word 'nout' doubtless being one of extensive signification in the colliery country, from which this witness comes."

The fame of Handley Cross rests on its rough, rowdy horseplay in the true to life tradition of English comic fiction. It is packed with real comic characters, pulsating with life, with Surtees 'gift for comic dialogue and wide knowledge of and ability to use slang and exaggerated invective. It also contains many hunts brilliantly described. Surtees had a great inventive genius and every hunt is different and never boring.

Handley Cross was followed by many famous sporting novels — *Mr. Sponge's Sporting Tours*, 1849; *Ask Mamma*, 1857; *Plain or Ringlets?* 1859; *Mr. Facey Romford's*

Shark and Chizeler were a greater menace than the thieves they were supposed to catch. As Surtees remarks of one of them, "He who couldn't control himself was placed in authority over others. He had a capital berth of it, having no one to look after him, and took his salary as a sort of retaining fee, looking upon 'incidentals' as he elegantly called his extortions, as the real emoluments of his office."

In *Young Tom Hall* Surtees has a scathing description of the Yeomanry or "cart-horse cavalry" as he called them.

"The facilities of railways enabled many listless, lounging, London bucks to bebeard and bespur themselves, and take up their quarters at his noble mansion for fourteen days, eating and drinking and playing at soldiers in the park. His lordship, who had the soul of an army tailor in the body of a nobleman, spent endless time and countless cash in the advancement of this his favourite hobby; and though in reality commanding but one regiment, it was as good as having two, for they were heavies in the morning and hussars at night. Red coats and horse-haired helmets, with leather tights and jackboots, were the marching order, while richly silver-braided, ermine-trimmed, lavender-coloured jackets and pelisses, and the aforesaid marmalade-coloured tights, with silver-tassel'd Hessian boots, annihilated the ladies of an evening."

Surtees was fascinated with the railways and the immense changes they brought in the social life of the country. His knowledge of dress, both male and female, was immense and the social historian will find his book an inexhaustible mine of information.

"Lord Lonnergan was one of a now nearly bygone generation, whose antiquity is proclaimed by their dress. He wore a large puffy shirt-frill and a puddingey white tie with flowing ends, a step collared buff vest, and a blue coat with white buttons. He had long adhered to tights and Hessians, and it was only when he found himself left alone in his glory that he put his fat legs into trousers. He was a porcupine-headed little man, who tied his cravat so tight as to look as if he were going to throttle himself. He was a short, sallow plethoric, wheezing, scanty-whiskered man, with eyes set very high up in his head, like garret windows; a long unmeaning-looking face, surmounted with a nose like a pear. His mouth was significant of nothing except an aptitude for eating. As we said before, he had a voluminous bouble-chin."

Surtees had little contact with workers. He did however understand servants — of whom there were thousands in his days, and he always described them as chiefly engaged in robbing their masters which they achieved with great skill.

Surtees died on March 16th, 1864 and is buried in Ebchester churchyard. His death was almost unnoticed. The local paper reported the event in 10 words, thus dismissing the greatest writer, after Bede, that the north has produced. Few guide books since, few works on local history, no local newspaper article have referred to Surtees. Truly a prophet is without honour in his own country.

Hounds, 1864. They are all still read today while many famous writers of his time are now forgotten except by literary historians.

Surtees was an extremely close observer of the life around him and often critical of the society in which he lived. Surtees was a landowner, one of the small squires then numerous in the north, but was unsympathetic to the aristocracy. The Duke of Donkeyton (a portrait based on Hugh, third Duke of Northumberland) is described without the least restraint. "The Duke," he wrote, "was a muddle-headed, garrulous old Whig — liberal, levelling, and mankind-loving out of doors — exclusive and a bit of a bashaw within."

"Donkeyton Castle," he wrote, "was clear of railways. You could not hear the sound of a whistle on the calmest day or with the most favourable wind. The Duke had a great dislike to them —'monstrous dislike'. Would have thought the Constitution destroyed if one had come near him — not his own constitution, but the constitution of the country." The judiciary, the police and the Yeomanry were all criticized umercifully. Superintendent Constables

Contemporary drawing from Illustrated London News showing arrival of foreign workmen at Newcastle

THE ENGINEERS' NINE HOURS STRIKE

In 1871 a strike of great significance, nationally as well as locally, took place on the North East coast Together with the famous miners strike of 1844 it illustrates the social struggles arising from the impact of the industrial revolution In all industries at that time hours were long and conditions of work generally deplorable by modern standards In many trades during the decade 1860 to 1870 a demand for the Nine Hours day had arisen and among the building workers had already been won. In Newcastle it took the masons a strike of 11 months to win the boon for Tyneside. Already in 1866 the Tyneside engineers had agitated for such a concession; but a sudden trade depression with its consequent unemployment had killed the movement.

Among engineers the Tyneside was considered a blackspot at this time. Although on the Clyde engineers' hours were 57 per week, and in London $58\frac{1}{2}$, on the Tyne they were 60. This comparative backwardness can be partly attributed to the weakness of the trade union movement. During the sixties there had been a remarkable expansion of the iron shipbuilding industry on the Tyneside, and thousands of workers unused to trade unionism had been brought into engineering, and although at a later date the Tyneside was to become well organised in a trade union sense, at that time barely 20% of engineers were in trade unions. But the workers of the area were traditionally militant, and they were uninfluenced by the conciliatory tactics then prevalent in most craft unions.

It was in Sunderland that the first moves were made under the leadership of Andrew Gourlay, President of the local branch of the Amalgamated Society of Engineers. Gourlay was a striking personality long prominent in trade union struggles. Victimized in the fifties for trade union activities in Crewe he had emigrated to the North East and started work in Palmers of Jarrow, where he was the leader of the workers during the lock-out of 1865, and the agitation for the nine hours day in the following year. Sacked by Palmers for his trade union activity Gourlay, after a spell of unemployment, obtained work in Sunderland.

In 1870 the Newcastle "Central District Committee" of the A.S.E. had once again discussed the Nine Hours Day, but taken no action. Suddenly on April 1st, 1871, under Gourlay's leadership, without the knowledge or sanction of the Executive Council, all Sunderland engineers came out on strike for the Nine Hours Day. In spite of being condemned "for their hasty action" by the District Committee, and contrarary to the expectations of the Executive Council who were for arbitration and a compromise, within a month the Sunderland engineers won a complete victory, with their full demands satisfied. The Sunderland strike was a remarkable piece of organisation and though Gourlay never became a national trade union

26

figure he had shown qualities of leadership which he was content to employ on a local scale. After this strike he drops out of history.

It was clear that a victory in Sunderland would stimulate the movement in other areas of the North East and accordingly on April 8th while the Sunderland strike was still in progress the master engineers of the whole district met in Newcastle to plan for a united resistance to the men's demands. Sir William Armstrong, who played a vital part in the development of the Tyneside engineering industry, was the leader of the employers.

Simultaneously as a result of deputations from Sunderland the Newcastle engineers were on the move. As the Sunderland strike was nearing a successful conclusion on April 29th an historic meeting was held at the Westgate Inn, Newcastle, consisting of elected representatives from practically all the engineering shops of the Tyne to plan the formation of a Nine Hours League. Learning from the experiences of Sunderland the Nine Hour League embraced unionists and non-unionists alike and to all intents and purposes was a temporary Trade Union with almost one hundred per cent membership. John Burnett, then the youthful secretary of one of the Newcastle branches of the A.S.E., and later General Secretary of the whole organisation, was chosen President.

Within a few days the engineering industry of Tyneside was in the grips of a strike in which 7,000 men struggled for nearly five months until the employers conceded the Nine Hour Day. The most spectacular feature of the strike was the attempt to break it by the use of imported foreign labour. Here is James Jeffries, the historian of the industry, in his work "The Story of the Engineers", describing what happenened:—

"It was in August that the employers started to introduce foreign workers into the shops. In an effort to prevent them from meeting the strikers they were lodged in the different factories and the schools belonging to Sir William Armstrong were closed to the children and converted into barracks for the foreigner. Tenants living in Sir William's property received notice to quit if they did not return to work; the various foremen and clerks who would consent to the operation were sworn in as special constables, and preparations were made to guard the different factories much the same as if they were convict establishments".

"Despite the fact that violence against the foreign workers was to all intents and purposes confined to speeches, the employers used the new Criminal Law Amendment Act to intimidate the men. So wide were its terms, that one young man was fined half-a-crown for 'looking at some foreigners smoking', and Margaret Monaghan, aged thirty three, got 21 days' imprisonment for 'hooting', the Mayor remarking 'that if women take the part of men, and he might say, would make themselves men, they could not wonder if they received the same as men'."

"The Nine Hour League, however, adopted effective means of ridding Newcastle of the foreigners. When the importation of foreign workers was still a rumour John Burnett was delegated to attend the Council meeting of the International Workingmen's Association in London. This body had been formed in 1864 and included on its Council not only Karl Marx but many of the leading trade unionists in Britain . . . Mr. Cohn, the Secretary of the Danish section of the International, was sent to dissuade Belgian workers from responding to the invitations of the Newcastle employers whose agents

Plate commemorating the engineers'
victory produced by a Gateshead Shop

Print 1839

were posting notices in the large cities of that country. Cohn replied by counter-notices and meetings. But he was not allowed to continue his work for long. The Belgian authorities yielded to an unseen pressure and expelled him. Returning to England, he was sent to Newcastle by the A.S.E., 'and by the manner in which he induced foreigners to leave Newcastle he was of great service to the cause."

"The work among the foreigners, despite the employers' precautions, was pursued to such effect that on August 30 occurred a 'mutiny' of 120 of the Germans employed in Armstrong's factory. All the efforts of the heads of the firm were insufficient to quell the disturbances; they promised that the Germans should be allowed to smoke when they chose; that in fact they should have everything but the nine hours, which the Germans had by this time begun to shout for. The Nine Hour League took

advantage of this state of affairs and the next day shipped off nearly the whole of the 120 . . . amid such a scene of excitement as is seldom witnessed.' And at a mass meeting held on the Town Moor on September 2, 'a large quantity of foreigners were on the platform expressing by signs their desire to go back to their own country'."

The strike was successful and before long the nine hour day was nationally recognised in the engineering industry. A sideline of the strike was the attempt by some of the men to open a co-operative workshop. The Ouseburn Engine Works was opened under the management of the Rev. Dr. Rutherford, after whom Rutherford Grammar School is named, and 300 men were employed there by the end of the strike on the nine-hour system. The venture however did not last long. After four years it closed down, in 1875, because of difficulties over wages and finance.

NEWCASTLE OFFICE.
25 MOSLEY STREET.

Queen's Head Inn.

28

DRINKING FOUNTAINS

Until the 20th century most people in England obtained their water from wells, pumps, drinking fountains and conduits. Providing drinking fountains was considered an act of charity and the names of benefactors can often be found on them. Not only people but animals, especially horses, needed to drink so means to do so were provided on most roads. Many of these old fountains have survived and provide picturesque street furniture. They are never identical. Their variety is remarkable. Those surviving reflect the individuality of their builders.

Drinking fountain and trough at Bamburgh probably made from fragments from an ecclesiastical building.

An old Bigg Market Pant, Newcastle.

A drinking fountain from Cambo c1880. The dolphin was on the Trevelyan coat of arms.

A dual purpose pump on College Green, Durham. Its water supply came from the fine 18th century Conduit House which stands nearby.

A Romanesque clock tower, drinking fountain and horse trough, Tynemouth.

Pump erected by the Temperance Movement — Pelican Band of Mercy, January 5th, 1889. One of several erected on road from Allendale to Catton especially for lead carriers.

NOTICE.

FREQUENT Complaints having been made to us of the Conduct of many young Persons, who assemble in different Parts of this Town, and particularly in the Market-Place, in the Evenings, and greatly annoy and disturb the Passengers and Inhabitants by the most tumultuous behaviour; we have strictly charged the Constables to be alert in suppressing such disgraceful Proceedings, and to take into Custody all Persons in future so offending.

The Constables having (in Virtue of their Office) Power to call upon any Person to assist them in quelling Tumults, we deem it proper to caution Persons against refusing their Aid when so required, as they will subject themselves to legal Proceedings for such Refusal.

ROBERT GREEN. } *Magistrates.*
NICHOLAS FAIRLES, }

Town-Hall, 28th October, 1818.

PAXTON, PRINTER, SOUTH SHIELDS.

FIVE GUINEAS
REWARD.

WHEREAS early on *Sunday Morning*, the 12th Instant, some evil disposed Person or Persons pulled down the PANT near Mr. Swan's, in the Fish Market, North Shields.

A REWARD of *Two Guineas* will be paid by the North Shields Water Work Company, and a further REWARD of *Three Guineas* by the North Shields and Tynemouth Association for prosecuting Felons, to any Person or Persons who shall give such Information as may lead to the Conviction of the Offender or Offenders.

North Shields, July 13, 1818.

W. BARNES, PRINTER, HOWARD STREET,

Nicholas Fairles was the magistrate allegedly attacked and murdered by William Jobling in 1832 at Jarrow Slake.

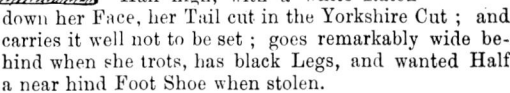

'Stolen or Strayed from Rothbury, on Thursday the 4th of September 1783 A light bay Mare, six or seven Years old, about 14 Hands and a Half high, with a white Ratch down her Face, her Tail cut in the Yorkshire Cut ; and carries it well not to be set ; goes remarkably wide behind when she trots, has black Legs, and wanted Half a near hind Foot Shoe when stolen.

Any Person who will give any information or bring her to George Fletcher, in Rothbury aforesaid, shall be handsomely rewarded for their Trouble, with all reasonable Charges paid.'

NORTHUMBERLAND GRAVE DIGGERS

At a meeting held on 13th April, 1658 in the church at Rothbury in Northumberland it was ordered:

"That no Grave be digd within ye Body of the Church under the price of five shillings. Because it being not flagged it would not only spoile the seates and floore, but endanger ye people's health by infectious Ayre, and Secondly, which may hinder Them at least in the service of Almighty God, for we see many have fainted and Swooned in the Church, which caused their Departure and often became The Beginning of a Tedious Sickness."

31

By courtesy of Morgan and Brown Ltd.

THE "WELLESLEY" TRAINING SHIP

This fine painting of Alexander Young (1896) shows the Wellesley Training Ship anchored off North Shields. For many decades this ship was a familiar sight on the Tyne. B. Plummer in his book — *Newcastle upon Tyne its Trade and Manufacturers*, 1874, has the following interesting description of this ship and its history.

Shortly after the passing of the "Industrial Schools' Act of 1866," Mr. James Hall called a meeting in Newcastle to consider the question of establishing a Training Ship on the Tyne. Such marked success had rewarded the managers of ships for the reformation of convicted criminals, that there was no difficulty in enlisting the sympathies of the public in a scheme for making sailors out of lads who were not yet criminal, but likely to become so. £3,000 was subscribed on the spot, and the Admiralty was applied to for the loan of a ship. Their lordships offered the "Diana," 42 gun frigate, but the School Ship Society of London, after ten years work, having obtained a larger ship to replace the "Cornwall," 50 gun frigate, the Committee succeeded in getting the reversion of that vessel on very advantageous terms. In July, 1868, she was named the "Wellesley," and inaugurated as the Tyne Training Ship, by his Grace the Duke of Northumberland.

In 1873 the "Wellesley" was overcrowded with 250 boys on board, and there being a demand for trained lads far exceeding the supply, the Committee were obliged to follow the precedent of the London Society and apply for a larger ship. The Admiralty replied that no line of battle ship could be spared, but at last granted the loan of the "Boscawen," on account of her being partially rotten. This ship, now called the "Wellesley," has been fitted out at a cost of about £3,500, a considerable portion of which has been spent in removing the infected portion of her timbers. The system of ventilation, devised by Mr. John Glover, is a novelty on board a training ship — instead of heating the vitiated air by means of hot water pipes, the air is drawn in from the outside, warmed, and distributed over the ship.

The material the Committee have had to deal with has been of the roughest and most unpromising kind. The numbers discharged on account of disease show that no selection has been made — they have never refused a boy. The results are, therefore, the more satisfactory.

The boys receive a practical education in school in the six standards approved by the Government code, with history, geography, etc. They cook the food, make all the clothing and boots, make and repair sails, mats, rope etc.; are exercised at sail drill, company and battalion manoeuvres, single stick, and dumb bell exercise, to which rifle drill is to be added. Their whole life, on board and in the boats, is a training for sea. Shortly before their time is up, they go to regular seamanship instruction — comprising knotting and splicing and wire rope in all its branches, compass and rule of the road at sea, lead and log line, rocket practice, etc.

When a boy's time is up, he generally ships as ordinary seaman, at 30 shillings a month, his outfit being provided by himself, for every facility is given to enable the boys to earn money to provide for their start in life; thus, some accumulate upwards of £5, others 5s. Many lads who have left the ship are now in receipt of upwards of £4 a month.

From July, 1868, to the present time, 505 boys have been received from the undermentioned places:—

Newcastle	 142	*Sunderland* ..	.. 31
North Shields	.. 112	*London* ..	.. 86
South Shields	.. 69	*Other places*	.. 38
Gateshead ..	.. 27		
		Total ..	.. 505

There were 272 on board in July, 1874. Of the 233 discharged, 18 have left on account of disease, 3 absconded, 3 transferred to other schools, 9 died, 5 sent to reformatories, and 11 returned to friends. Of the remaining 184, nearly all have gone to sea, and the rest have been provided with situations on shore—the latter, almost invariably, are prevented going to sea by their relations, and, as frequently go to sea a few months after leaving.

The results are on the whole most satisfactory, and if the boys were only up to their age in size and weight, would be still more so. Some ships take them voyage after voyage; sometimes they ship as able seamen in their second voyage.

The "Wellesley" and her sister training ships claim to be in a way towards solving some of the gravest difficulties of the present time. By taking the children of the very lowest strata away from their evil associations, they cut off the supply of criminals from the gaols and paupers from the workhouse. They save the lives of hundreds of children; they clothe, feed, and educate, and then turn them out into the mercantile marine with a technical training to be got, nowadays, nowhere else but in a training ship.

North Shields. 1882

The Wellesley had been a ship of the line and was a five decker. When she first arrived on the river she had the wooden warship Caster for company. This is probably the other ship shown on the picture. On March 11th, 1914 fire started on the Wellesley and she was destroyed. The figurehead of the Wellesley, an effigy of Admiral Boscawen is preserved at the present headquarters of the school at Blyth.

LOW LIGHTS, NORTH SHIELDS, 1895.

The first Lowlight at North Shields was built in 1540. The present High and Low Lights were built in 1805-8 and first lighted on 1st May, 1810.

ROGER THORNTON

Roger Thornton who died in 1429 was a great benefactor of Newcastle. He is often compared to Dick Whittington because he arrived in the town as a poor youth and became its wealthiest citizen. The chronicler Stowe says he entered Newcastle with only "a happen hapt in a ram's skin," His wealth was derived from the trade which he carried on with the Continent and from the lead and silver mines he owned in Weardale. It was due to his influence that in 1400 Henry IV made Newcastle a city which placed it outside the jurisdiction of the sheriff of Northumberland.

His great gift to Newcastle was the *Maison Dieu* (House of God) which stood on the Sandhill near the present Guildhall. It was dedicated to St. Catherine, and founded in 1412, for the care of nine poor men and four poor women. His son later granted to the town the use of the hospital, hall and kitchen "for a young couple when they were married, to make their wedding dinner in, and receive the offerings and gifts of their friends, for at that time houses were not large." Adjoining the Maison Dieu was the Town House which Bourne also claims was built by that "worthy man Roger Thornton".

When his wife died in 1411 he commissioned Flemish engravers to carve a magnificent monumental brass to her memory. It was originally part of an altar tomb which was ruthlessly destroyed when the original All Saints was demolished. The brass survives and is in the present All Saints' Church. Thornton and his wife are drawn life-size. There are ninety-two figures on the brass including their fourteen children together with saints and angels.

Lead Poisoning.

Sources of Disease and Means of Prevention.

Water is the means of transit by which all food is conveyed into and through the system, the medium in which all physical functions are carried on, hence any impurity which it contains is almost necessarily borne to the seat of the most **vital functions.** It is rarely supplied pure, either in town or country.

Water is generally supplied through **lead pipes** and thus becomes liable to poisonous contamination. The softer the water the more likely is it to dissolve an amount of lead from the pipes.

THE
Mawson Filters
Supply Absolutely Pure Water
Free from Poisonous Lead Salts.
Free from Disease Germs and Organic Impurities.

Practical Advantages of the Mawson Filter :

There is no possibility of unfiltered water passing.
No skill is required to renew the Filtering Medium.
They are simple, reliable, and give no trouble in use.
They can be taken entirely to pieces to be cleaned.

Manufacturers :

The MAWSON FILTER Co.
Newcastle-on-Tyne.

Although the water supply in working class areas was deficient and often unclean in the late nineteenth century, the middle classes of Newcastle were conscious of the need for themselves to drink and surprisingly were aware of the danger of lead in the water supply. Hence the popularity of Mawson's Filters which are now collectors items.

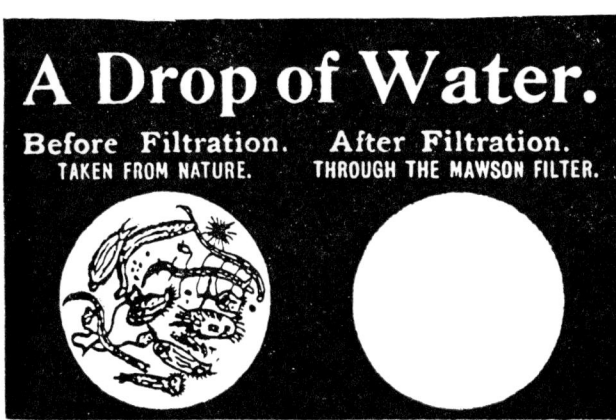

A Drop of Water.

Before Filtration.   After Filtration.
TAKEN FROM NATURE.   THROUGH THE MAWSON FILTER.

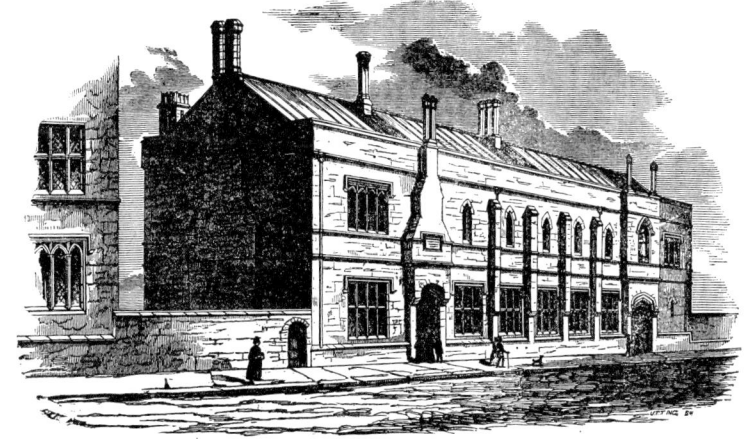

NEWCASTLE-UPON-TYNE COLLEGE OF MEDICINE,
IN CONNECTION WITH THE UNIVERSITY OF DURHAM.

MARKET PLACES

The market place is still today one of the most interesting parts of many northern towns and villages and some are still used on certain days for trading purposes. A hundred years ago they were much more important centres of trade and commerce. In a series of old engravings and more modern drawings we show some market scenes which have survived until today with little change while others have altered almost beyond recognition.

Market Place and Entrance to the Castle Grounds, Bishop Auckland. 1895

BELFORD

The market at Belford is long obsolete but the market cross survives. It is a tall square pillar with a modern head standing on two worn steps.

Belford Market Place 1920 by Hugh Thomson

Belford Market Place c.1908 from photograph

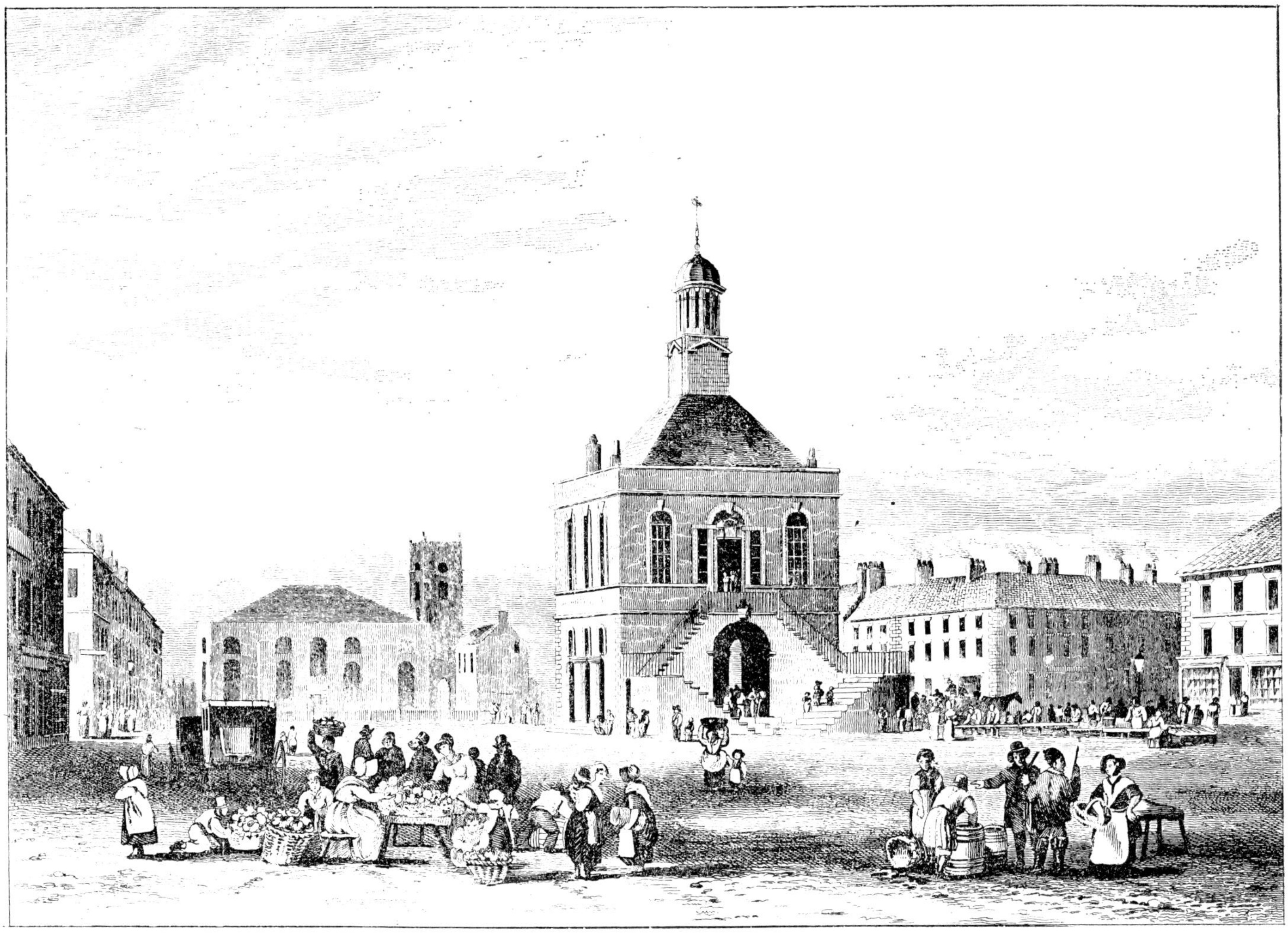

South Shields Market Place by W. Galland 1800

SOUTH SHIELDS

It is not known when the first market was held in South Shields. In the Middle Ages the law in England stated that markets must be a distance of six miles from one another. However Newcastle claimed that the law did not allow any market to be established within a radius of twelve miles of Newcastle. This claim led to continual disputes with North and South Shields.

However there are occasional early references to the Shields market. In 1634 four men who had abused the constable and watch were flogged in public fastened to the end of a cart and drawn round the Market Place which would then be in the old High Street. In 1662 Richard Parke was fined 12d for the crime of *forestalling the market by buying a bowl of oatmeale before the townspeople could have liberty to be served with itt, and for selling it again immediately att excessive gaine to the prejudice of the poore.*

In 1768 the present Market Place at South Shields was built. Prior to the enclosure of the Market Place a weekly market had been held in the crooked, narrow street along the river-side in the eastern part of the town.

In order to provide offices for their officials and to shelter the market people the Dean and Chapter of Durham erected the building known as the Town Hall or the "Cross" in the centre of the Market Place. The builder was a local man called Hunter. The central pillar of the building is supposed to have been the original market cross. It bears on its north side the inscription, "Durham $18\frac{1}{4}$ miles".

At the same time as the Market Place was developed the town was granted the right of two annual fairs, the first of which was held on June 24th, 1771. Today the market at Shields is held on Monday and Saturday.

The village of Westoe also had an early market and fair. They are referred to in a document of 1375.

BEDLINGTON

The market cross still stands. It takes the form of an obelisk. Its date is unknown but probably erected in the 18th century.

37

L. Dunn Delin.   Neele sc. London.

WEST SIDE OF THE MARKET PLACE STOCKTON

STOCKTON

Stockton has probably the largest market place in Britain and its market is famous. The first weekly market and annual fair were granted by Anthony Bec, Bishop of Durham, in 1310. The market day of Wednesday has continued down to the present time.

In 1834 the market is described as "abundantly stored with all kinds of grain, butcher's meat, fish, poultry, butter, eggs, vegetables etc. and attended by a host of hawkers, with their different sorts of wares." On one occasion a man auctioned his wife from a stall on Stockton Market. The woman was sold for 2s. 6d. The affair caused a great noise in the town.

In the centre of the High Street stands the Town Hall or Town House. It was erected in 1735 and enlarged in 1744 when the old Toll-booth was taken down. A little to the south of the Town Hall stands the Market Cross a handsome Doric column, 33 feet high, which replaced an old covered cross in 1768.

Blagroves House, Barnard Castle

38

MORPETH

The privilege of holding a weekly market on Wednesdays was first granted to Roger de Morlay by King John in 1199. From this beginning there developed the great cattle market which in the 19th century was the most important in Northumberland. The tolls of the market were frequently used for town improvements. In 1610 the "towle of this yeare comeing to £12 3s. 6d was bestowed upon the newe waye at the bridge". In 1612 the "toule for this yeare amonted to £11 2s. where of £7 10s. 6d was expended in making of courses in the towne streat". When John Hodgson wrote his history of Morpeth in 1832 "every horned beast coming into the market payed 1d; every score of sheep, 4d; every pig and calf, ½d; and the widows of poor freemen had a dishful of corn for every poke set upon the pavement for sale". The weekly sale of oxen averaged 200 and sheep and lambs 2,500. Most of them came from Northumberland and Scotland and many went south as far as Leeds, Manchester and London.

The well known view of Morpeth Market by Thomas Allom shows the cattle and general market taking place together.

The Market Place is dominated by the Town Hall which was erected originally in 1714 on the site of the old Toll Booth from a design by Sir John Vanburgh. It was however entirely rebuilt in 1870 from the plans of the Newcastle architect R. Johnson. The facade is an exact reproduction of Vanburgh's design. Adjoining the Market Place is the old Clock Tower. The two illustrations of the Market Place are by Charles Harper, 1900, and Byron Dawson, 1957.

THE MARKET HALL AT BARNARD CASTLE

This quaint octagonal structure standing in the middle of the street was built by Thomas Breakes in 1747. It replaced the old tolbooth which stood at the opposite end of the Market Place. The Doric columns round the base support a veranda which was used as a market for dairy produce. The piers supporting the upper structure were enclosed to form a lock-up. Stairs lead to the hall which was used as a court-room and town hall. Here the town records were kept. The turret above the roof houses the town's fire bell. The 18th century fire engine which used to be housed in the Market Hall was used to deluge John Wesley when he preached outside. Finally the building is crowned with a weather vane which has two bullet holes in it. These were caused by two local marksmen who were competing for a wager in 1804. They fired from the Turk's Head which was 100 yards away.

The engraving above is from William Brown's "History of the Parish of Ryton" 1896

Below: the sign of the Hat and Feathers, Durham 1900.

Below: Durham Market Place 1830

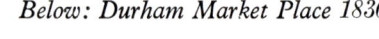

DURHAM

Durham Market Place though somewhat small in area contains some interesting buildings and is attractive in appearance. On the north side is the colossal bronze statue of the third Lord Londonderry by Raffaelle Monti. Behind is the rebuilt church of St. Nicholas. On the west side is the old Town Hall. It was erected and given to the city by Bishop Tunstall about the year 1555. In 1752, 1754 and 1849 the edifice was enlarged and restored. In the north

west corner used to stand the palace and gardens of the Neville family. This 15th century building was demolished in 1851 and replaced by the New Market "constructed somewhat after the manner of a railway station."

Due to the control of the bishops Durham city was never able to develop commercially in the same way as Newcastle. Hence its markets and fairs were never so important as many others in the north.

Our illustration of Durham Market Place is from an extremely rare print. Except for the one in my collection I have never heard of another. Its date is about 1800. In front of St. Nicholas' can be seen the piazza. A large market cross was erected in 1617 by Thomas Emerson of London whose arms were placed on the west side. It had a large pillar in the middle ornamented with a dial but it became ruinous and was demolished in 1780. The materials were used in building this piazza which was used as the market for corn and provisions. The piazza was demolished when Lord Londonderry's statue was erected. Also can be seen the market pant where there was a fountain of excellent water. The fountain has existed since 1450. The reservoir is octagonal and adorned with a statue of Neptune which was placed there in 1729. Like so many secular buildings in Durham this has also disappeared. To the right of the fountain is the famous old hostelry of the Hat and Feathers displaying its signboard. Needless to say it no longer survives. *Market day at Durham is now on a Saturday.*

Market Place, Durham

41

At Sotheby's sale in 1974 it is described as follows:—

"A John and George Angell interesting and large tea kettle on lamp-stand, complete with detachable burner, the triform base engraved with inscription and supported on scrolling feet, the stand with applied aprons engraved armorials, the otherwise plain compressed circular kettle with ovalo collar, melon finial, and swing handle, makers mark, London, 1849, the under side of the base struck with the makers mark of William Burwash and Richard Sibley, London 1806."

The history of the kettle is very obscure, even the person who sold it at Sotheby's is unknown. The two date marks show clearly the kettle was either extensively repaired or altered in 1849. In 1886 it was found in the possession of a prominent pawnbroker of Canterbury Alderman Hart. It was bought by John Clayton who wrote an article about it in *Archaeologia Aeliana* (1889). From that time nothing is known of its history.

Cuthbert Collingwood was born on October 24th,

THE COLLINGWOOD KETTLE

On numerous occasions the Council of Newcastle presented objects of silver to people whom they wished to honour. On almost every occasion such gifts were made in London although Newcastle was well known for its skilled silversmiths. The silver soup tureen presented to Richard Grainger is an example as well as the silver kettle here 1748 in a house at the head of the Side. Our illustration shows the brick fronted house in the centre next to the Burns Tavern. His father was a merchant who had become bankrupt a few years before his birth. Young Collingwood was educated at the Grammar School of Newcastle and started his naval career at the age of thirteen. His subsequent career is well known and need not be repeated here.

In 1805 the Common Council of Newcastle decided to make a presentation to Vice Admiral Collingwood of a piece of plate to the value of one hundred and fifty guineas. The kettle was the gift chosen. It is inscribed in cursive letters:—

The gift
of the Corporation
of Newcastle upon Tyne
to their distinguished
Fellow Burgess
Vice Admiral Lord Collingwood
in testimony of their high Estimation
of his eminent Services to his
King and Country
in various Naval Engagements,
and especially at the memorable Battle off Trafalgar
on the 21st day of October, 1805,
when he gallantly led the Van of the British Fleet into Action
and after having succeeded to the chief Command
upon the glorious and lamented Death of
Vice Admiral Lord Viscount Nelson
completed the most brilliant decisive Victory
over the combined Squadrons of France and Spain
Henry Cramlington,
Mayor.

An original letter from Lord Collingwood to the Mayor of Newcastle, Mr. Cramlington, relating to the gift has survived. Here it is in facsimile.

Queen off Cadiz April 13th 1806 —

Sir

By my letters from Newcastle I am informed
that you have done me the honour to write to me a letter
to congratulate me in the name of the Magistrates & Corporation
of Newcastle on the Success of his Majesty's Fleet — in the
battle of October last — I have waited with impatience
for this letter, which would have much gratified me — to
receive the congratulations & good wishes of a Body I so
truly respect — and where I have so many personal friends
— yet, I have to regret it has miscarried — and not come
to me —   But understanding the purport of it to be
complimentary to me — I cannot delay to return my
sincere thanks for it — and for an Elegant piece of plate
they have presented to me — which as a token of the
esteem & regard entertained for me by that ancient &
respectable Body, I shall preserve an inestimable value
for —   I beg Sir you will please to make known to
my respected Townsmen, the high sense I have of the
honour they have done me, in the Interest they so kindly
take in my Welfare & Success — which I hope will attend

To The Right Worshipfull The Mayor of Newcastle —

44

John Dobson, Architect.   The Collingwood Memorial.   Now Building at Tynemouth.   F. Mackenzie.   Lith.

RALPH HEDLEY (*1849-1913*)

Ralph Hedley is one of the finest artists who have practiced in Newcastle. In his work he has recorded the life and work of the people of Tyneside. As times passes it will be realised that he was not only an artist but a social historian. He presents a most varied picture of ordinary folk at work and play. His canvasses show people poorly dressed in tattered clothes but people of character not painted wooden dolls. He depicted his contemporaries with sympathy and humour. His paintings are examples of social realism. The oil painting illustrated shows a boy making butter.

Ralph Hedley was born 31st December, 1848, in Richmond, Yorkshire and came to Newcastle early in his life. He was apprenticed to John Tweedy wood carver in Grainger Street. In St. Nicholas' Cathedral and many other places in the county Hedley's work as a wood carver can still be seen. He attended the old Newcastle Art School and the Evening Classes of the Life School, where he was taught by W. Bell Scott. He first exhibited at the Royal Academy in 1879 and his last contribution was an oil painting called *Weeding Potatoes* exhibited in 1913 at the Burlington House Exhibition. The Sandgate Clothes' Market was painted in 1896 and can be seen at the Laing Art Gallery. It is usually considered his finest work. Other important works many of which can be seen at the Laing include *The Sail Loft, Prisoners in the Tower, Passing the Doctor, The Veterans, The Market Waggons, The Sanctuary, The Sword Dancers, Proclaiming the Horse Fair at Corbridge, The Fisherman's Sunday,* and *Contraband.*

"Mr. Hedley holds certain opinions of his own as to the mission of the artist. He thinks that there are plenty of good subjects to be found in the North, and that it is unnecessary to go further afield. Moreover, he contends that an artist should give special study to events of our own day in preference to those which took place say a couple of centuries ago. This, he thinks, is the true ideal of the historical painter. That he carries out his views is proved by the subjects of his pictures".

The Monthly Chronicle 1889

HELL'S KITCHEN, NEWCASTLE

The famous Hell's Kitchen at the Flying Horse in the Groat Market has become a legend about which countless tales, true and untrue are told. In the Monthly Chronicle of 1888 a detailed account was given of this famous place which we here give in full:—

"The kitchen was situated in a yard on the opposite side of which were three other places of rendezvous. The three latter rooms were frequented by highly respectable people, while the kitchen itself was the 'beat up' of beggars, tramps and loafers.

One of the places mentioned was known as the 'printers' room.' Here gathered, night by night, the literary element of the town in that day; hither came, fresh from the theatre, the critics of the time to state their solemn judgment on the play of the night; and associated with them were a mixed multitude, distinguished for their aptness at song and recital.

We leave this apartment for what has been described to us as 'a kind of miscellaneous room.' Here the company was mixed indeed; but there was nothing to complain of in their general behaviour. They did not profess to be saints; but, to give them their due, they were not such very good sinners.

And then there was the 'old men's room.' It may seem a strange regulation, but nevertheless it is true; no smoking after four in the afternoon was allowed in this room. The old boys didn't like the fragrant weed; and the law was laid down accordingly. Each of the veterans had his own seat, his own hat-peg, and his 'surroundings comfortable,' as an old play says.

The 'vestry' was situated behind the bar. To obtain admission therein was somewhat of a task; the admission itself was a privilege. In front there was the 'cocked hat room,' so called because there was a peculiarly-shaped table therein, a sort of triangular affair, which suggested the name to those who settled the affairs of the nation in its vicinity.

The kitchen proper had its whims. One of them was to elect a mayor for the due control of the proceedings during the municipal year. His worship was elected with all form and ceremony, and of course he was 'on hospitable thoughts intent' when duly elected. He invited his loyal subjects to dinner. First course: fish. When that was disposed of, up got Mr. Mayor and said, 'Well gentlemen, you seem to have enjoyed the fish so much that I'm certain you want nothing more excepting the beer. Order accordingly. Now this magnificent first course was — a red herring! When 'Jack Huntley,' however, was elected mayor, he made an innovation in this respect He gave his supporters a glorious spread in the shape of some three or four plucks and a sufficiency of liver and bacon. 'Jack' — there are some amongst us who still remember him — went to China, whence he sent to Newcastle a descriptive letter in regard of his new surroundings which, by its graphic pictures-quences, considerably surprised his old cronies of the kitchen.

It need hardly be said that so peculiar a company must have had a curious mortal as its controlling head. And Ralph Nicholson, the landlord, was equal to his surroundings. He had his rules, and he stuck by them. If anyone transgressed, the worthy Ralph suspended him from further attendance for six calendar months, at the end of which time the offender was required to report himself, and promise better behaviour. In one instance, an offender, having stayed away for the regulation half-year, walked into the kitchen. Ralph could not tolerate this 'Have you reported yourself?' 'No.' 'Then come this way.' Away went the landlord to the door with his truant customer, and said: 'Now, do you report yourself?' 'Yes, certainly.' 'Walk in.' Such was the discipline of the kitchen! Nicholson had considerable dignity of his own; his successor, Liddle by name, was more — what shall we say? — more 'come-at-able.' He was usually referred to as 'His Satanic Majesty!' Yet according to all accounts, he was a law-respecting citizen, who could give a joke and take a joke as well as any of his neighbours.

More might be said concerning this almost historic house; but we must pause. We must not dwell on the 'safe pints' — the 'printers' by the way, were always supplied with pints, and nothing else — and we must reluctantly leave 'Auld Nick's Visit to Hell's Kitchen' as described by Robert Emery, alone. We ought, however, to explain that the reason for the name quoted is that some rough customers used to find their way to Ralph Nicholson's premises now and again. They waxed fightable in their cups, and he would lock them in, and leave them to fight their difficulty out, having always, though, a leaning to the weaker vessel! In other words, he always took care to interfere before any serious mischief was done. In the veritable kitchen, which was the tap-room of the Flying Horse, the poker — a formidable instrument — was chained to the fireplace, lest it should be used in a quarrel; and so we have seen it. There are, however, old veterans who dispute the chained poker altogether; but we think that our story as

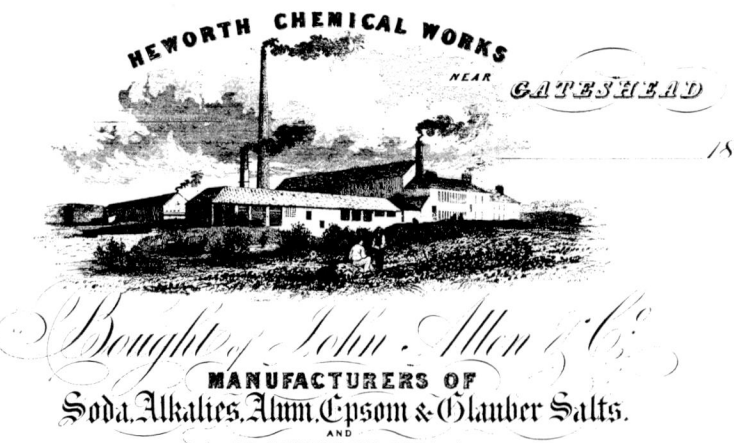

to the three rooms, the cocked hat, the vestry, and so forth, may sufficiently, and very reasonably, account for that."

Hell's Kitchen has been immortalised in a famous painting by Henry Perlee Parker. The original oil painting has disappeared but an engraving by George Armstrong and published by E. Charnley, whose famous bookshop was a few yards away in the Bigg Market, has survived. It is called the *Eccentric Characters of Newcastle upon Tyne* and was issued in 1820. It was once extremely popular and could be found displayed in countless houses in Newcastle. The central figure is the singer "Blind Willie" surrounded by thirteen cadgers, tramps and Newcastle eccentrics.

The Flying Horse was demolished many years ago to make room for Thomson House.

Kilhope Lead Crushing Mill, Weardale

The above engraving c.1930 shows the "Flying Horse"

CHOLERA
Morbus.

THE London Gazette of FRIDAY, contains an Official Document, issued by the Board of Health, for the prevention of this Dreadful Disorder, the **MAYOR OF NEWCASTLE**, particularly requests, that the Inhabitants of this Town, and more especially in the narrow Chares, and Streets, will observe the greatest CLEANLINESS, and that they will open their **WINDOWS**, and Ventilate their Houses, during the Day.

Mansion House,
Oct. 24th, **1831.**

J. Clark, Printer, 11, Newgate Street.

DOUBLE EXECUTION AT DURHAM.

TRIAL AND EXECUTION OF

M'CONVILLE & DOLAN

For the Murder of Philip Trainer, of Darlington, and Hugh John Ward, of Sunderland, in the County Prison, at Durham, on the 22nd instant.

Yesterday the two murderers, Dolan and M'Conville, were executed within the precints of the goal at Durham. M'Conville, who who was 23 years of age, worked as a furnace-man at Darlington, and was convicted of the murder of Philip Trainer, on the 30th of January last, Dolan murdered a man named Hugh John Ward, at Sunderland, on the 8th of last December. The two convicts left the condemned cell shortly after eight o'clock, each supported by a couple of warders, and attended by the Rev. Canon Consett and Rev. G. Waterton, Roman Catholic priests. A procession, headed by the under sheriff, moved to the west wing of the prison, where the scaffold was erected. The warders conducted the men chained from their cells, and they were taken through the corridors to the pinioning room, where Calcraft commenced his duties. Both men submitted quitetly, and prayed unceasingly with the priests. Canon Consett ministered to M'Conville, and the Rev. Waterton to Dolan. At 6 minutes to eight the prison bell began to toll, the hour had scarcely struck before the outer door of the pinioning room opened and the procession issued into the inner court of the prison. It passed along a narrow passage between two wards and abruptly turning to the left, come into the open work yard, where the low gallows was erected. In passing across the yard neither criminal seemed to notice the slight swelling among the cinders and gravel close to their path, which indicated the spot where their graves already dug were lightly covered until the tenants for them were ready. Close to the gallows Calcraft stepped forward and conducted M'Conville under the beam. The criminal was deadly pale, but with upright bearing and steady steps advanced without faltering, Calcraft completed his work in full view of Dolan, who shuddered perceptibly, but never ceased joining in the prayers & responses with the Rev. Waterton. At length Calcraft finished with M'Conville, and then conducted Dolan under the beam. In a few seconds this convict was made fast to the beam, the Clergy and Calcraft crept off the drop, and while petitions for mercy were spoken aloud by both the victims, the bolt was drawn. Dolan died almost instantaneously, but M'Conville struggled for several seconds. After hanging an hour the bodies were cut down, and an inquest was held at eleven.

COPY OF VERSES.

A double murder we have to tell,
  Most dreadful to relate,
Dolan and M'Conville named,
  Who met an awful fate.

Philip Trainer, of Darlington,
  Was by M'Conville slain;
And Hugh Ward, of Sunderland,
  Dolan murdered in the lane.

Two Roman priests attended them
  In prayer the night before,
Who begged for mercy from on high,
  And their sad crime deplore.

At eight o'clock precisely,
  The prison bell did toll;
Each being led and supported,
  Under the warders' controul.

Where the gallows was erected,
  And loosened from their chains;
Their graves too was constructed,
  To receive their sad remains.

Within the prison they met their fate,
  Now according to the law;
And Calcraft performed his duty,
  For crimes mankind abhor.

A black flag was hoisted,
  On the prison walls,
Denoting all was over,
  The death that men appals.

May the Lord have mercy on their souls,
  For their most dreadful crime;
And a warning let it be all
  To the end of time.

W. Smith, Printer, Lincoln.

THE
Whittle Dean Water Company

CAPITAL £150000 IN SHARES OF £25 EACH

THE SEAL OF GATESHEAD HOSPITAL.

THOMAS BROWN,
Ship Builder,

EAST HOWDON DOCK, SLIPWAY & GRIDIRONS
WEST HARTLEY STAITH,
near NEWCASTLE ON TYNE.

JOHN WOOD,
STEPNEY POTTERY,
NEWCASTLE-UPON-TYNE.

MANUFACTURER OF THE FOLLOWING :—

WHITE, PRINTED, SPONGED, PAINTED, CANE, ROCKINGHAM,

AND EVERY DESCRIPTION OF

BROWN EARTHENWARE,

FOR HOME AND EXPORT.

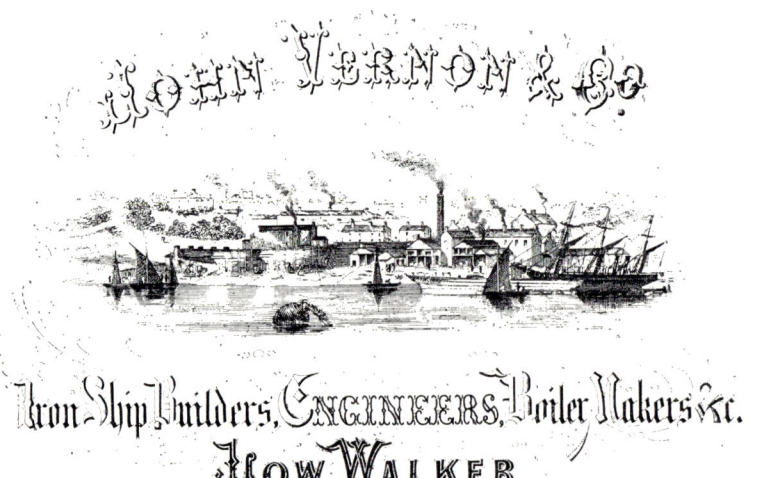

JOHN VERNON & Co

Iron Ship Builders, Engineers, Boiler Makers &c.
LOW WALKER.

BOOKPLATES

Bookplates, or "ex-libris", as they are sometimes called, are labels pasted inside book covers to designate ownership. They have been used in Britain from the 16th century, printed by all the different methods of printing popular at the time. They are important for artistic and historical reasons. Some provide us with important biographical information.

The earliest north country bookplate is almost certainly that of Robert Trollap of York and Newcastle. Trollap is one of the earliest known Newcastle architects who was admitted a freeman of Newcastle in 1657. He completed the building of the Exchange or Guildhall in the same year. He certainly built Capheaton Hall and probably Bockenfield Manor House, Callaly Castle, Netherwitten Hall and Swarland Old Hall. He was buried in St. Mary's Churchyard, Gateshead.

In the second half of the 18th century many bookplates came from the Beilby and Bewick workshop. They were known especially for their landscape vignettes. Bewick himself personally engraved three or four "ex-libris" but he may have assisted his apprentices in the numerous designs which came from his workshop. It is estimated that about ninety surviving designs came from the Bewick workshop but is doubtful whether the master helped in more than a few of them.

The bookplates were however typical of the period and similar in design. "Very charming," wrote Warren (1880) are their *ex-libros* vignettes. They show us ruins, rocks, deep foliage, or time-corroded boles, flowing river distant spire and mountain. They give actual Tyneside scenes, views of Newcastle, St. Nicholas's Tower, Jarrow Church. Unluckily the armorial shield is far too often present,

Robert Trollap (of Yorke and Newcastle, Free-Mason) his Booke, 1657.

intruding itself into fishing-scenes and similar incongruous situations. But for this, the orderer of the book-plate rather than the engraver was to blame."

The earliest dated *ex-libris* was, for T. Bell, 1797. One of the most interesting was that for "Swanley (Richard), Newcastle". Motto: "Libertas auro pretiosor". Two female figures with cornucopia, shield, cap of liberty, etc. *Copper-plate.*

(The book label of Robert Trollap is from *Early Printed Book Labels* by Brian North Lee. 1976)

THE KEELMEN'S STRIKE, 1822.

THE KEELMEN OF TYNESIDE

Keels and keelmen were peculiar to the Tyne in the early days of the coal trade. The word keel comes from the Anglo-Saxon word "ceol." meaning a boat. They have probably been used on the Tyne since the days of the Anglo-Saxon invasions, and the keel used in the coal trade in the 18th century differed little from the ships in which the Scandinavian rovers sailed far and wide in search of plunder.

The keels were used to carry goods from the shore to ships lying in the middle of the river, and although used for all kinds of merchandise they were chiefly engaged in conveying coals, the main trade of the Tyne.

There are various references to the use of keels in the 14th century, and in 1516 the keelmen are mentioned as a craft. They eventually became an independent society, but due to the opposition of the Hostmen, as the coal-owners were then called, they never became an incorporated company.

The keelmen lived as a separate community in the Sandgate, and due to the nature of their work, inter-marriage, and long traditions, they considered themselves as a class apart. But they always played an important part in the life of Newcastle. In times of danger they were always to the forefront in defending the city. In time of social strife they were always active in defending their own interests and those of the rest of the common people, whilst in times of festivity the Sandgate, down by the Quayside, was the liveliest part of old Newcastle.

Only the strongest of men could manage the keels, and although in other trades the inhabitants of Scotland, Tynedale, and Redesdale were frowned upon, they worked in considerable numbers in the keels. The crew of a keel consisted of a skipper, two "keel-bullies" — bully being here used not in the derogatory but in the Anglo-Saxon sense of "beloved" — and a boy called the "Pee-Dee."

The keelmen were employed by the fitters of the collieries near the Tyne, and as with the miners they were "bound" for one year. Binding day was at Christmas, and prior to the great strike they were given a gratuity of one guinea and a supper on being bound. Part of their pay was in beer, and in one of their strikes they complained about the quality of the beer provided at the can-houses. They termed it "savage", saying that "while it was only fit for savages they were charged the gentleman's price for it."

The keelmen, although living before the days of modern trade unionism, were always united in defending their interests. Many were the strikes in which they took part, and whenever force was used against them they could always retaliate.

In the books of Gateshead Parish Church, under the year 1671, we find an entry — "Paide for powder and match when the keelmen mutineyed, 2s."

In those days to go on strike was to mutiny against the established order. In times of distress, when the people of Newcastle were suffering from hunger, the keelmen were always in the van in the struggles of the poor. In the hard

THE Civil Authorities regret to find the deluded Keelmen still continue to insult His Majesty's Boats, by throwing Stones when protecting those that are willing to work ; and finding Forbearance any longer will endanger the Lives of those so employed,—This is to caution the peaceable Inhabitants, and Women, and Children, to keep within their Houses during the Time the Keels are passing from the Staiths to Shields, as the Marines have Orders *to fire on the first Man that shall dare to throw a Stone at them.*

November 22nd, 1822.   G. Angus, Printer, Newcastle.

winter of 1739-40, when people were dying of hunger, the keelmen led a great demonstration into the Guildhall, where they broke open the "Town's Hutch," as the chest where the money was kept was termed, and distributed the contents of £1,200 among the needy.

They were liberal with their money when they had it, and often openly irreligious. But they led the way in the whole country with regards to the provisions they made for their aged and sick brethren. As early as 1700 they had agreed that one penny per week be deducted from their wages for this purpose, and in the following year they increased the levy and built the famous Hospital which still stands in City Road. However, as with many working-class charities, they were not allowed by law to run the hospital themselves, but the coal-owners assumed this right, although on many occasions the keelmen complained that they could have done the job better themselves.

The great strike of 1822 was the last of the great struggles of the keelmen and the beginning of their end as a fraternity. The strike was doomed to failure because in essence it was a fight against the new techniques brought in by the Industrial Revolution which was then in full stride on the Tyne.

Although there were many matters in dispute in the strike, the main question was the use of the staithes at which ships were now coaling without the use of keels. The keelmen saw that the staithes would ultimately deprive them of their livelihood. They had protested against them in the strikes of 1708 and 1794 and earlier, when Charles I was passing down the river from Newcastle to Shields, they had presented a petition to him against the staithes.

Both sides in the struggle — the keelmen and the coalowners — presented their case to the public in broadsheets. Besides objecting to the staithes, the keelmen complained of reduced wages, non-payment of binding money, and the breakdown of the old system of being bound three months before their engagement ended, so that they did not know till the last minute whether they would have work for the next year.

They also protested against the "press gang," because although in time of peace the keelmen were exempted from the press gang, because of the national importance of the coal trade, in times of war they were in great demand since they made fine sailors.

The strike was conducted with violence. Pitched battles took place at North Shields, Scotswood, and in the Castle Garth. Those who had taken part in the riots were hunted down by the authorities, assisted by a strong body of special constables. The military were brought into the area in large numbers, and seven men-of-war lay in Shields Harbour during the strike.

On this occasion the keelmen received the support of the seamen of the river. The seamen had been on strike seven years earlier in 1815 on account of unemployment, and had attempted to form a union to fight for increased manning scales and increased pay. This strike had been broken by the civil authorities, assisted by the navy and military. During this period they were putting up a grim struggle against the shopowners, and three years later, in 1825, they were able to form their first union — the Loyal Standard Association.

With the assistance of the seamen the keelmen were able to prevent ships coaling at the staithes. The marines were unable to manage the keels, and the only keels which ran the blockade were those towed by the "Tom and Jerry." This was one of Hedley's locomotives from Wylam colliery, which was put on a keel, fitted with wheels as paddles, and used as a tug.

The strike lasted for ten weeks but ended without the keelmen attaining their main objectives namely, the limitation of coal loaded at the staithes. The only concession granted was that the Pee-Dee was replaced by a man, but since the men on the keel were paid on a co-operative basis, it merely helped unemployment by a reduction in wages.

Failing in the strike, the keelmen took their case to law. Maintaining that the spouts were a public nuisance, they brought a charge against a representative of the Wallsend Colliery. The case, "Rex versus Russell," was tried in August, 1824, at York. The jury returned a verdict of not guilty. The keelmen were dissatisfied with the verdict and brought the case up twice more without success.

Steadily the keelmen's trade declined. The openinig of the Swing Bridge in 1856 opened up the higher reaches of the river to large ships. In 1872 the yearly binding was abolished, and by the end of the century keels were rarely seen on the Tyne.

TYNESIDE'S PROTEST AGAINST MASSACRE OF PETERLOO

In 1819, as a result of an economic crisis, the movement for political Reform and the repeal of the Corn Laws developed to new heights. Huge meetings were held all over the North and Midlands. One such meeting took place on the 16th August, in St. Peter's Fields, Manchester. 80,000 people assembled to hear the famous Radical, "Orator" Hunt. The magistrates sent the Yeomanry — armed Tory volunteers — to arrest the speaker. The Yeomanry had difficulty in getting through the dense crowd and the cavalry were ordered to charge. The people were driven off the field with the Yeomanry hacking indiscriminately with their sabres. Eleven people were killed and several hundred wounded.

This brutal attack on a peaceful crowd, and subsequent defence of the action by the Government, were regarded by the workers as a declaration of war against themselves. "This one dramatic scene revealed like a flash of lightning the real relation of rulers and ruled", as Trevelyan puts it.

The indignation aroused was widespread Meetings of protest were held throughout the country. One of the largest was held in Newcastle. Here the Reformers had an organisation called the "Political Protestants", which had been established when Major Cartwright visited the area in October 1815. This group had done little till the economic crisis of 1819, which, as the local historian Eneas Mackenzie noticed, rendered the workers "sober and thoughtful". Mackenzie tells how "numerous reading parties associated to trace the causes and the cure of their sufferings in the cheap Registers of William Cobbett, the "Black Dwarf" of Jonathan Wooler, and other popular writings of the same kind."

The Political Protestants increased in numbers and began to meet regularly in classes of twelve, each member (unless unemployed) paying a penny a week.

Immediately on receipt of the news of "Peterloo" (as the Manchester massacre was scathingly called) the old unreformed Town Council of Newcastle sent a message of congratulation to the Prince Regent and promised to deal with the forces of "anarchy and atheism" in Newcastle. But the people of Newcastle thought otherwise, and the United Committee of Political Protestants decided to call a protest meeting on the Parade Ground.

The Whole of Tyneside responded, and from all areas they marched in with banners flying and bands playing. Behind the Union Jack at half-mast, the societies marched four abreast, arms linked, their leaders bearing white rods crowned with crape. Other banners bore the words: "Truth, Order, Justice"; "We'll brothers be for a' that"; "May Justice overtake the Manchester Murderers". Bands played "Rule Britannia", and "Scots wha ha'e . . ."

The Parade Ground soon became too small and for an hour and a quarter the demonstrators marched past Barras Bridge to the Town Moor, where 80,000 people eventually gathered. Resolutions were passed protesting against "the outrage at Manchester", claiming "the rights and liberties of Englishmen", and promising financial support to the victims of "Tyranny and Oppression". The meeting passed off without violence because of the remarkable discipline of the people, and the non-appearance of the military whom the Mayor wisely kept away. So disciplined were the men, we read, "that a division of seamen from Shields drunk nothing but water during the day, and passed the ale-casks on the road-side without regret."

The Mayor, like the rest of the richer class in Newcastle, was scared by the demonstration, as can be seen from a letter he wrote to the Home Secretary, Viscount Sidmouth, six days after the meeting:

"It is impossible to contemplate the meeting of the 11th inst. without awe, more especially if my information is correct, that 700 of them were prepared with arms (concealed) to resist the civil powers. These men came from a village about three miles from this town; and there is strong reason to suspect that arms are manufactured there: they are chiefly forgemen."

The Mayor was correct. These men of Winlaton, popularly known, from the place of their employment, as "Crowley's Crew", were well armed. Not only had they manufactured pikes in large numbers and primitive hand grenades, but they had made caltrops (known locally as the "craa foot") — four-pronged instruments which,

IT being thought expedient, at this Period, by many of the Inhabitants of this Town, to form an ARMED ASSOCIATION, for the Protection of Property, in Aid of the Civil Power; such Persons as wish to enrol themselves, for that Purpose, are informed, that they may enter their Names and Places of Residence in a Book, which will lie at the Exchange, Sandhill, until the 28th Instant in the Evening, when the List will be closed.

Newcastle, 25th October, 1819.

G. Angus, Printer, Newcastle.

REFERENCE.   *Proof*

1. Mr. MACKENZIE .... 4. Mr. THOMAS HODGSON. 7. Mr. JOB JAMIESON...... 10. SHORT HAND WRITERS.....

2. Mr. MARSHALL .... 5. THE REV. Mr. MACPHERSON. 8. Mr. WEATHERSTON ...... 11. The Distance exhibits the orderly

3. Mr. LAYTON................. 6. Mr. STEPHENSON......... 9. Mr. CAMPBELL......... Manner of the Procession.........

This Meeting was held to consider the outrage committed at Manchester on the 16th of August 1819. It was convened under the auspices of the Reformers, and with the consent of the Mayor. The Reform Societies walked in procession, four abreast, under direction of their leaders, who carried white rods surmounted with crape. Each division was distinguished by a splendid banner or flag, and some of them were preceded by a person carrying a Roman fasces. Several bands of Music played popular tunes, and imparted order and interest to the procession, which was one hour and a quarter in passing the Barras Bridge, from which circumstance it was inferred, that above 25,000 men were in rank. The space occupied by the compact body of the meeting was measured, and would hold 76,000 persons, at the rate of four to a square yard. The shouts of this multitude were so tremendous, that a Partridge, flying over their heads, dropt down dead with the shock. The whole was conducted in the most admirable order.

however thrown, had one spike upwards to pierce the feet of horses and so make cavalry ineffective. These stern measures of the Winlaton men made a repetition of Peterloo impossible in Newcastle, and on many other occasions the presence of "Crowley's Crew" prevented interference by the authorities.

The response to the meeting so alarmed the authorities that special constables were sworn in and a Volunteer Corps of Cavalry was formed to combat the Reformers, the Corporation providing £100 for their equipment.

However, the Corps did not prove very popular. We are told that "they were subjected to many taunts and sarcasms and distinguished by the scoffing appellation of NOODLES".

In the political ferment of those times Newcastle and the towns round about teemed with pamphlets and tracts on the question of Reform (Mackenzie gives details of twenty-nine). Petitions were circulated, placards posted and handbills distributed. And so, stimulated into mass action by the massacre of Peterloo, Newcastle played its part in the fight for Reform.

SELLING PICTURES

Old engravings are today very popular. They are outstanding examples of the work of artist craftsman. Unfortunately the lithographic reproductions, so common today dismally fail to recapture the fine craftsmanship of the original engravings. They reduce a crisp clear picture to a soft muddy caractures. Engravings can be divided into four main categories namely woodcuts, copperplates, lithographs and steel engravings. Most of the original prints that we see today were engraved on steel. Since the plate did not wear out quickly steel plates could be used for several thousand copies unlike copperplates which deteriorated after a few hundred copies were run off.

In the 19th century engravings were mainly used for book illustrations and steel was the main method employed. The small topographical steel engravings were all book illustrations and those on sale today have unfortunately been taken from books of topographical views.

However a number of engravings, particularly large ones, were specially produced for sale as individual prints. They were often sold in limited edictions at what were high prices (bearing in mind the value of money at that time). These large prints are much sought after. They are rare and sometimes bring large prices. The advert we reproduce advertises one of these large local views. From it we can learn much about marketing art in the nineteenth century.

Many local artists, notably J. Carmichael and T. M. Richardson painted views intended for reproduction. In our book, Historical Newcastle, can be seen several of these prints in colour.

In the 19th century local artists flourished in the north. They were the product of a growing and wealthy industrial society. They painted for a local market which they knew and which knew them. They had few national and no international competitors. There was none of the artificial spearation of the craftsmen from the artist which is so prevalent today.

ST. NICHOLAS' CHURCH, NORTH VIEW

Robert Johnson was born in 1770 at Shotley, a village in Northumberland, and became an apprentice to Beilby and Bewick. He proved a poor engraver but a fine painter in water-colours. The design for several of the tail-pieces in Bewick's Birds and the drawings for most of the woodcuts in Bewick's Fables were his work. He died in 1796 at the early age of 26.

His fellow apprentice at Beilby and Bewick was Charlton Nesbit who was born at Swalwell in the county of Durham. During his apprenticeship he engraved some of the tail pieces in the first volume of British Birds. He was undoubtedly one of the best engravers of his time. Shortly after completing his apprenticeship he decided to engrave a large cut which is illustrated above, from a drawing by his friend Robert Johnson. It is probably the largest cut ever engraved in England. Including the border the cut is fifteen inches wide and twelve inches high. Twelve pieces of box had to be used, well cramped together and mounted on a plate of cast iron. The completed work won a medal from the Society for the Encouragement of Arts and Manufactures. Woodcuts were rarely used for topo-graphical views since large cuts were difficult to engrave. Lithographs and later steel engravings were the conventional mediums employed.

The picture of St. Nicholas is of great historical interest. All the secular buildings in the view disappeared long ago. In 1838 Middle Street was demolished removing all the buildings on the right of the engraving. This created a grand view of St. Nicholas from the wide curve of the Bigg Market. Unfortunately despite some opposition including that of John Dobson and Richard Grainger this view was blocked in 1858 by the erection of the Corn Exchange and the Bigg Market. When a few years ago this group of buildings was demolished the view was opened again but for "financial" reasons a group of nondescript modern buildings replaced the old Town Hall.

The carriage on the engraving would be a private one. The hackney coach wasn't introduced to Newcastle until 1824. They occupied a stand near St. Nicholas. Before the sedan chairs were the main method of "general" conveyance.

On the left of the picture is the lower part of the Cloth Market which was removed when Moseley Street was built. Part of it survives in St. Nicholas' Square.

JAMES ALLAN, THE GYPSY PIPER

Jemmy Allan the gypsy piper was famous in his lifetime and a legend after his death. Several books, one an octavo of 480 pages, were written about him and his aprocryphal adventures. Today he is almost forgotten.

He was born at Woodhouses, near Rothbury, in March 1734, one of a family of six gypsy children. A local squire seeing he was a bright child arranged for him to attend school but he could not endure the discipline and left. He then enlisted in the band of the Northumbrian Militia at Alnwick but found it worse than school and deserted. To avoid arrest for desertion he wandered around Northumberland making his living by playing the pipes with robbery as a side line. All accounts describe him as an accomplished musician and in 1769 he became one of the town's musicians at Alnwick. He only held the position for a short while before he was dismissed from his post and he resumed his life of a wandering gipsy piper. He was twice arrested and charged with felony but won acquittal. In 1803 he made his last theft. He had been playing at the Dun Cow Inn on Newcastle Quayside and after leaving he crossed the river to Gateshead where he stole a horse. He made for Border but was followed and arrested. After his trial at the Assizes he was condemned to death, a sentence which was commuted to transportation. But he was too old and ill for the sentence to be carried out and spent the rest of his life in prison where he died on 13th November, 1810.

RIDING THE STANG.

NEWCASTLE'S FIRST CINEMA SHOW

Our picture shows the first recorded cinema show in Newcastle on the Town Moor. It is Mander's Royal Waxwork Show and Edison's Electric Animated Pictures at the Fair in 1904. It was the fairgrounds which first brought "living pictures" to the people of Tyneside.

There is much controversy as to the place where the first cinema in Britain was established. In the provinces the original tin Olympia in Northumberland Road was one of the first, if not *the* first, regular cinemas.

"The Olympia had been used as a Music Hall in place of the Empire in Newgate Street, during its rebuilding in 1902/3. *Empire at Olympia — Trams pass the Door* ran the bills. The proprietor, Edward Moss and Richard Thornton closed down the Olympia when the new Empire opened 14 December, 1903. It was immediately leased to Ralph Pringle, trading as the North American Animated Picture Company, a condition of the lease that Variety acts formed no part of the programme. As far as is shown, this building remained a cinema until its destruction by fire in 1907."

Picture Pioneers by G. T. Mellor

Sir Oswald Stoll who ran the Stoll Picture Theatre in Newcastle from 1918 and had interests in film studios in the London area.

Our forefathers realised the dangers of excessive drinking but did not understand the harm done by smoking. The two woodcuts are adverts for tobacconists made in Bewick's workshop.

WAR DECLARED!!
60,000 SLAIN!
ANNUALLY.

The Public of South Shields are invited to attend the

SEAMEN'S HALL, FOWLER STREET,
ON TUESDAY EVENING, JAN. 31, 1854,
WHEN

MESSRS. ROBT. ALLEN & THOMAS HANLEY

WILL PROVE TO THEM THAT STRONG DRINK IS MAN'S GREATEST ENEMY.

Mr. Holmes, of North Shields, will Recite some interesting Pieces. N.B.—The Temperance Choir will be in attendance to enliven the Meeting.

Chair to be taken half-past Seven o'clock.

PRINTED BY COXON AND CO., 3, WEST KEPPEL STREET, SOUTH SHIELDS.

South Tyneside Public Libraries and Museums

FIREMARKS

Firemarks were instituted by insurance companies to identify buildings at a time when such companies maintained their own fire brigades. So when a fire involved several buildings the fire brigade would know which building to concentrate on. After the fire services were municipalised in the 1830's the need for such marks gradually disappeared but they were still used for advertising purposes. In some areas the insurance companies amalgamated for the purpose of firefighting. Firemarks are usually of lead, copper or cast iron. Where the insurance records have survived companies can trace which house was covered by a particular mark by its number.

A number of buildings still have their firemarks on the wall. The Craster Arms at Beadnell has the lead sign of a Newcastle Insurance Company with insignia of three castles and the number 7058. Glanton has numerous firemarks on its houses, perhaps more than any other Northumbrian village. Firemarks are now collected and the rare specimens fetch high prices. This has led to the unscrupulous production of forgeries.

The Darlington mark is in sheet iron and is dated 1907-1914 (Bulau 1017). It is produced by permission of Phillips Auctioneers at whose London salerooms regular sales of firemarks are held. The smaller illustration with the name Newcastle belongs to the Commercial Union Assurance Company. It is extremely rare and was originally issued by the Newcastle upon Tyne Fire Office (1783-1859). It is a convex oval of thick copper. The other Newcastle mark is made of lead and belongs to the author.

The three illustrations are approximately half the size of the originals.

61

PENSHAW MONUMENT

This is probably the most conspicuous monument in the county of Durham and a building of great interest. It is a great pity that it has been allowed to fall into a state of dilapidation and urgently needs repairing. It was built in 1844 to the memory of John George Lambton the Earl of Durham. Lambton was an enlightened man and for his day a radical politician. The design of the monument is copied from the Temple of Theseus but the dimensions are double the original. The length is 100 feet, width 53 feet and height 70 feet. John Lambton was born in 1792 and died in 1840. When the foundation stone was laid we are told 30,000 assembled to witness the ceremony. In the nineteenth century buildings of all kinds were opened with great pageantry and large crowds present. The picture was drawn by J. C. Farrow and also shows Lambton Castle and the Victoria Railway Bridge.

(We understand the National Trust is now repairing the monument).

THE LAMBTON WORM

The story of the *Worme of Lambton* is one of the most popular traditions of County Durham. This story has been handed down by oral tradition through many centuries. The song, however, which we know today is not very old, since it was first used in a pantomime at the old Tyne Theatre in 1867.

ONE Sunday mornin' Lambton went a-fishin'
  in the Wear;
An' catched a fish upon he's heuk,
He thowt leuk't varry queer,
But whatt'n a kind ov fish it was
Young Lambton cuddent tell.
He waddn't fash te carry'd hyem,
So he hoyed it in a well.

Chorus:

Whisht! lads, haad yor gobs,
An' Aa'll tell ye aall an aaful story,
Whisht! lads, haad yor gobs,
An' Aa'll tell ye 'boot the worm.

Noo Lambton felt inclined te gan
An' fight i' foreign wars.
He joined a troop o' Knights that cared
For nowther woonds nor scars,
An' off he went te Palestine
Where queer things him befel,
An' varry seun forgat aboot
The queer worm i' the well.

But the worm got fat an' growed an' growed,
An' growed an aaful size;
He'd greet big teeth, a greet big gob,
An' greet big goggle eyes.
An' when at neets he craaled aboot
Te pick up bits o news,
If he felt dry upon the road,
He milked a dozen coos.

This feorful worm wad often feed
On caalves an' lambs an' sheep,
An' swalla little bairns alive
When they laid doon te sleep.
An' when he'd eated aall he cud
An' he had had he's fill,
He craaled away an' lapped he's tail
Seven times roond Pensher Hill.

The news of this myest aaful worm
An' his queer gannins on

Seun crossed the seas, gat te the ears
Ov brave an' bowld Sor John.
So hyem he cam an' catched the beast
An' cut 'im in twe haalves,
An' that seun stopped he's eatin' bairns,
An' sheep an' lambs and caalves.

So noo ye knaa hoo aall the foaks
On byeth sides ov the Wear
Lost lots o' sheeps an' lots o' sleep
An' leeved i' mortal feor.
So let's hev one te brave Sor John
That kept the bairns frae harm,
Saved coos an' caalves by myekin' haalves
O' the famis Lambton Worm.

  Noo lads, Aa'll haad me gob,
  That's aall Aa knaa aboot the story
  Ov Sor John's clivvor job
  Wi' the aaful Lambton Worm.

SHOTLEY BRIDGE SPA

In the early nineteenth century there was a great development in health spas. There were many springs in the northern counties which were said to have healing properties but only Shotley Bridge Spa was properly exploited. For many centuries the Hally Well of Shotley was thought to be remedial in scrofulous complaints. As the old rhyme said

"No scurvey in your skin can dwell
If you only drink the Hally Well."

The actual spring had become overgrown but in 1838 a local Quaker called Jonathan Richardson cleared the site and erected a suitable building. "An upright stone was placed over the well and the water was made to flow through a spout into a round, low basin. A saloon and bath-room were erected a short distance off, carriage drives and footpaths were formed and soon the estate resembled an ornamental garden. To the south-east of the Spa, and in close proximity, a handsome hotel, planned on a large scale, with a suitable set of stables was built; and other residences starting into existence at the same time for the accomodation of the visitors who flocked to the place, the general aspect of the village rapidly changed."

The cures were soon taking place as testimonies abounded just as for patent medicines today. The spa claimed specially to cure *a tendency* to decomposition.

At Hamsterley Hall nearby lived Robert Surtees the famous sporting writer. His novel "Handley Cross" was based on Shotley Bridge and provided him with a golden opportunity to parody what he saw. He describes the enterprise of one Roger Swizzle a "roystering, red faced, round-about apothecary: Hearing of a mineral spring at Handley Cross, which, according to usual country tradition was capable of 'curing everything', he tried it on himself, and either the water or the exercise in walking to and fro had a very beneficial effect on his somewhat deranged digestive powers. He analysed its contents, and finding the ingredients he expected, he set himself to work to turn it to his own disadvantage . . . Being a shrewd sort of fellow, he knew there was nothing like striking out a new light for attracting notice, and the more that light was in accordance with the wishes of the world, the more likely was it to turn to his own advantage. Half the complaints of the upper classes he knew arose from over-eating and indolence, so he thought if he could originate a doctrine that, with the use of Handley Cross waters, people might eat and drink what they pleased, his fortune would be as good as made . . . Aided by the local press, he succeeded in drawing a certain attention to the water, the benefit of which soon began to be felt by the villages of the place; and the landlord of the Fox and Grapes had his stable constantly filled with gigs and horses of the visitors. Presently lodgings were sought after, and carpeting began to cover the before sanded staircases of the cottages These were soon found insufficient; and an enterprising bricklayer got up a building society for the erection of four-roomed cottages, called the Grand Esplanade . . ."

The opening of the Consett Iron Works soon ended the development of the Shotley Spa.

HAYDON BRIDGE SPA

One and a half miles down the Tyne from Haydon Bridge are the remains of the Spa, approached by a path from the Hexham road. All that can be seen today is a small basin in which water trickles. The spa was never able to develop.

Above Two Bewick blocks showing children at play

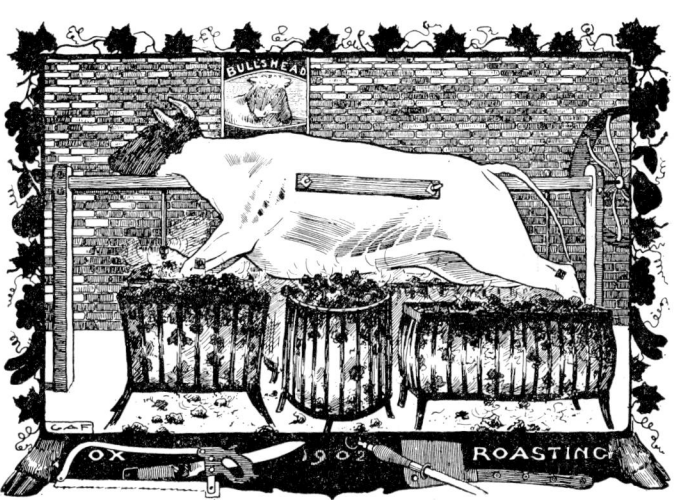

Ox Roasting Engraving commemorating an Ox roasting at Darlington held to raise money for the local hospital

THE SIGN PAINTER.

THE BILL STICKER.

THOMAS HEPBURN, *1796-1864*

One of the outstanding leaders of the working-class movement in Northumberland and Durham was Thomas Hepburn, a pioneer of trade unionism among the miners and an agitator for the People's Charter. Feargus O'Connor, who knew him well, described him as "a noble specimen of human nature, and the people of the North of England have a right to be proud of such a man".

Born near Chester-le-Street into a mining family he had to start work at the age of eight because of the death of his father in a mining accident. After working in various pits he is found in 1830 at Hetton Colliery where he was known as a "ranter". It was here that Hepburn made the first successful attempt to establish a miners' trade union. From the leading part he played in its formation it has always since been referred to as "Hepburn's Union".

As soon as the union was formed they began to demand the end of the Tommy Shop system (truck), reduction of hours of labour for boys (they worked 14-18 hours per day), end of evictions without process of law, and of arbitrary fines. The agitation led to a lock-out on Binding Day, April 5th, 1831.

All the forces of "law and order" were used to smash the union. But it was too strong and too well led. As a proof of Hepburn's influence over the miners the story is told that when a huge meeting was in progress on the Black Fell the Marquis of Londonderry came up accompanied by a military escort. His enquiry was 'Where is this great man of yours, your leader Hepburn?' and it was immediately concluded that he had come to take him prisoner. The assemblage was therefore thrown into great confusion and the consequences might have been serious had Mr. Hepburn lost his presence of mind, and betrayed either fear or resentment. But he coolly held his handkerchief up, the signal for order; and it was obeyed as implicitly as if he had been the general of a a perfectly disciplined force. The Marquis, who had seen a deal of active service, is said to have exclaimed when he saw this 'I never saw one man have so much influence over a body of men as this fellow has'." (Newcastle Weekly Chronicle).

The dispute ended in a spectacular victory for the men. They gained a twelve-hour day for the boys, and the end of the truck system. Hepburn was victimised because "he was the cause of all the mischief". But shortly after was appointed full-time union organiser. A few weeks later 12,000 miners gathered at their first political demonstration in favour of the Reform Bill.

Meanwhile the mineowners were preparing to smash "Hepburn's Union". At the Binding time in 1832 they refused to bind any union man. But the men "showed no disposition to leave the union at the behest of their employers ', and a great struggle was on.

The Home Secretary, Lord Melbourne, told the local magistrates to help in smashing the union. "All who hold the Commission of the Peace" were requested "to act with promptitude, decision and firmness which are so imperatively required, and that they will exert themselves for the prevention and suppression of all meetings which shall be called together for an illegal purpose, or which shall, in the course of their proceedings, become illegal; for the detection and punishment of all unlawful combination and conspiracy, as well as of all outrage and violence; and for the encouragement and protection of His Majesty's peaceable and well-disposed subjects."

After a struggle the union was broken. Many of the leaders who were "marked men" emigrated to Australia. "The last delegate meeting that was held was at the Cock Inn in the fore part of September, when Thomas Hepburn had the offer of £300 to set him up in business, as we all knew he would have to suffer. He refused it saying we would all have to suffer as well as him. We all did so, for shortly afterwards we (the delegates) got our leave from the coal trade and work was refused us at all the collieries; but I believe most of us got better situations, as many never went into the coal mines more" (Article in Weekly Chronicle, 1882).

In spite of his personal difficulties Hepburn was not downhearted In one of his last speeches at this period hes aid:

"If we have not been successful, at least we, as a body of miners, have been able to bring our grievances before the public; and the time will come when the golden chain which binds tyrants together, will be snapped, when men will be properly organised, when coalowners will only be like ordinary men, and will have to sigh for the days gone by. It only needs time to bring this about."

For a while Hepburn is little heard of. He worked at the Felling pit where we are told the viewer offered him work on condition he did not have anything to do with the union again.

On January 1st, 1838 he entered the struggle again as one of the founders of the "Working Men's Association". This organisation at first campaigned against the Poor Law. When Victoria was crowned they held a monster republican demonstration with 400 banners and 40 bands. Later in the year the Northern Political Union was formed to agitate for the People's Charter, and Hepburn was one of its best known speakers.

The Chartist movement on Tyneside reached its peak next year in July 1839 with the "Battle of the Forth". The authorities had decided to put down the movement with force. The miners' historian, R. Fynes, tells us that "Mr. Hepburn, the great man who had led the miners, was the only one who volunteered to oppose John Fife with the special constable, when the Riot Act was read over four times, and prevented them from holding their meetings. He stood on the wall and shouted with his strong clear, distinct voice 'John Fife, Mayor of Newcastle, I tell you your proclamation is no law. You have no right to prevent us from holding our meetings'."

Hetton Colliery in the time of T. Hepburn

THE PITMENS EJECTMENT, OR THE BATTLE OF FRIARS GOOSE.

Following the "Battle of the Forth" John Fife was denounced on all sides "as a traitor, a renegade, and a second Judas Iscariot", because of his previous associations with the Reform movement. With these denunciations still ringing in his ears he was knighted by the Queen "as a mark of approbation of the manner in which he had sustained the office of chief magistrate under very critical circumstances."

Although he lived 25 years longer, the words in which he denounced John Fife are the last recorded words of Hepburn. In Heworth cemetery a monument has been erected to his honour by the miners, and on it are these words:

"SHORTER HOURS AND BETTER EDUCATION FOR MINERS:

This stone was erected by the miners of the North and other friends, to the memory of Thomas Hepburn who died December 9th, 1864, aged 69. He initiated the first great union of northern miners in 1831, and conducted the strike of 1832 with great forbearance and ability. His life was spent in advocating shorter hours and extended education for miners."

Monument in Eardon churchyard in memory of the men and boys who died in the Hartley Pit disaster. January 16th, 1862.

The PITMEN'S UNION;
OR,
THE LADS
Of the Wear and Tyne.

NOW let the colliers' hearts be glad,
  While plenty round them shines,
And blest contentment flows along
  The banks of Wear and Tyne.
      CHORUS
  Still round our banners we will stand,
    In love and truth combine,
  And children yet unborn shall sing,
    The lads of Wear and Tyne.
Brave Hepburn and our delegates,
  Like rays of virtue shine,
Their fame shall long be echoed round
  The banks of Wear and Tyne.
On Bolden Fell our flags shall wave,
  Like victory's wreaths entwine,
But peace shall be the motto still,
  With lads of Wear and Tyne.
We envy not the rich and great,
  Whose dazzling greatness shine;
While we the hardy sons of toil,
  Can labour in the mine.
Our happy wives and children now,
  All former cares resign,
And sing with joyful mirth and glee,
  The lads of Wear and Tyne.
May he, who rides upon the storm,
  Protect with care divine,
From all the dangers that surround
  The lads of Wear and Tyne.
Here's a health unto the King,
  Likewise the Queen sublime,
Who gave the pitmen their applause,
  That dwell on Wear and Tyne
Now to conclude and make an end,
  May luck around them twine;
O, bless the happy collier lads,
  On both the Wear and Tyne.

Stephenson, Printer, Gateshead
July 1831

DOVECOTES

Dovecotes came to England with the Normans. In the Middle Ages food for cattle was hard to find in the winter. So in autumn most of the animals were slaughtered and the meat salted. Only those needed for breeding were kept during the winter. Salted meat is a monotonous diet so pigeons were kept so they could be used as fresh food when needed. Not everyone could have a dovecote. Only the landowners and church dignitaries were allowed to have them. Ordinary folks were banned from building them although the birds would get some food from their land and crops. Dovecotes are difficult to date but the early Norman ones were circular and very solid, built in stone. Later ones were more decorative, sometimes square and sometimes in brick with thinner walls. There are only a few dovecotes left in our two counties of which we give some examples.

GLANTON HOUSE DOVECOT

Homestead in Durham showing dovecot. 1877

Medieval Dovecote at Bamburgh, Northumberland.

Dovecote at Embleton

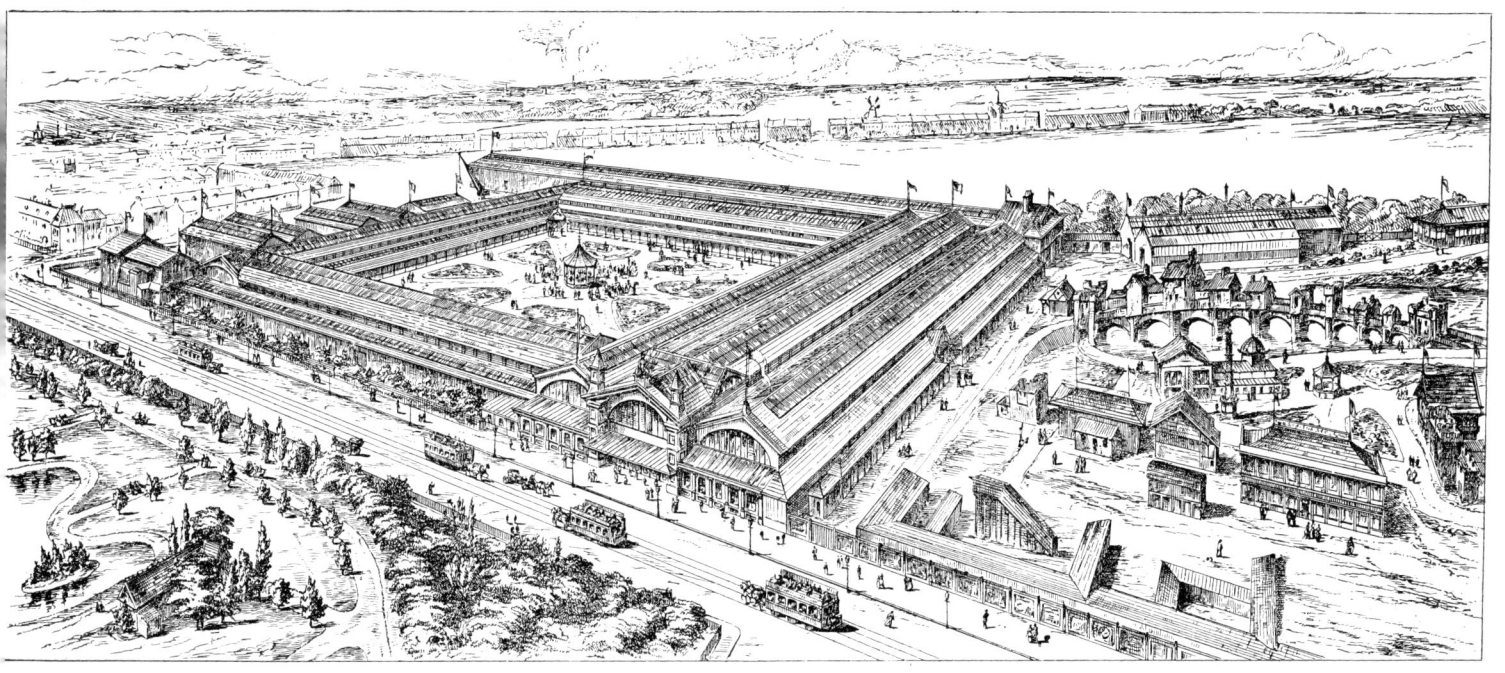

ROYAL JUBILEE EXHIBITION, NEWCASTLE-ON-TYNE.   OPENED BY HIS ROYAL HIGHNESS THE DUKE OF CAMBRIDGE, MAY 11TH, 1887.

ROYAL MINING ENGINEERING AND INDUSTRIAL EXHIBITION *1887*

In 1887 the Royal Mining, Engineering and Industrial Exhibition was held on the Town Moor in the area which from that date was called Exhibition Park. It was a magnificent show only rivalled by the North East Coast Exhibition of 1929. We are told that "among other great attractions are the Fine Art Gallery, Royal State Carriages, Collection of Indian Treasures, Large Working Models of Coal and Lead Mines, Old Tyne Bridge as it existed in the year 1770 with shops, forming then the main communication between England and Scotland. There was a Full sized Model of 110 ton Gun and a complete Exhibition from the Elswick

Works, the Northern Arsenal—Model Working Bakeries and Dairy—Military Engineering Encampment—Two Bands and Grand Organ Recitals daily—Tobogganing Slide, 360 feet long—312 acres of Ground, all of which with the Building, is brilliantly illuminated by the Electrical Light."

The 1929 Exhibition was on a larger scale. It lasted six months and attracted almost 42 million visitors. One of the buildings, the *Palace of Arts*, now the Museum of Science and Engineering, remains to remind us of this great event. (See *The North East Coast Exhibition of Industry Science, and Art. 1929.* by Christopher Baglee. Pub. Frank Graham 1979).

THE KITTY   STAMFORDHAM

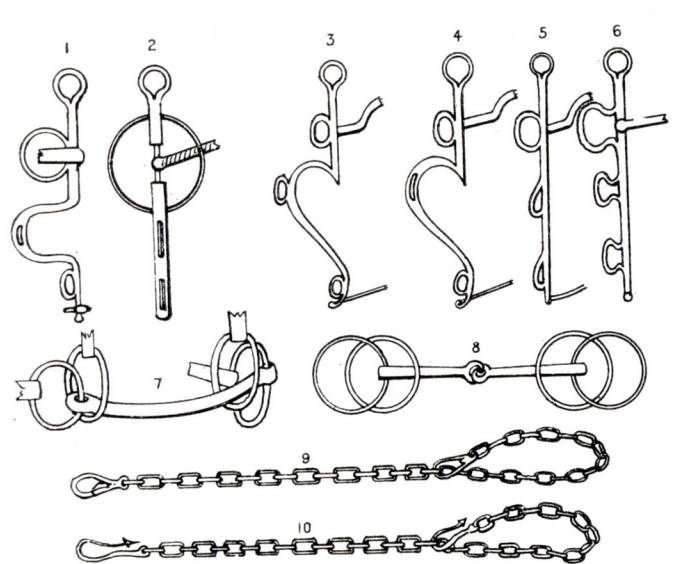

Mounting Block outside *Lion and Lamb*, Horsley.

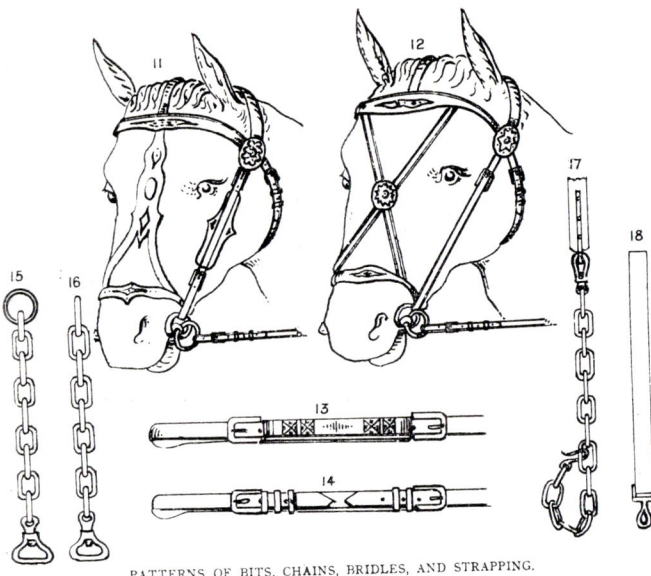

PATTERNS OF BITS, CHAINS, BRIDLES, AND STRAPPING.

Advert for horse harness made by John Philipson of Newcastle
1882

The Stables at Chollerton Church

THE HORSE IN THE NINETEENTH CENTURY

Before the invention and development of the internal combustion engine the horse was an integral part of our civilisation. Without it the standard of living would have declined dramatically. The photographs and drawings on this and the previous page show some interesting aspects of the horse in the 19th century.

The Stables

Lighthouse on North Pier at Sunderland 1841.

Mechanics' Institute, Houghton-le-Spring.
Artist H. Richardson. Lithographer I. Storey. Published by R. Turner, Gray Street, Newcastle, 28th May, 1852.

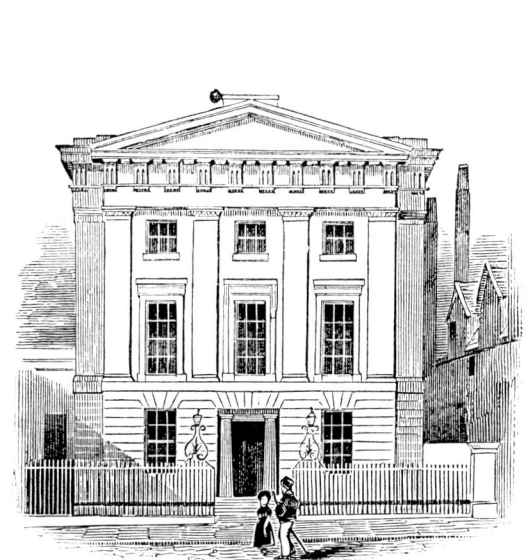

THE NEW BUILDING OF THE LITERARY AND PHILOSOPHICAL SOCIETY (1826).

STUPENDOUS RAILWAY ARCH OVER DEAN-STREET, NEWCASTLE-UPON-TYNE.

Tyne Theatre
c. 1910

From an engraving by I. D. Watson, 1860's artists' impression of first people saved from the "Tenterden" of Sunderland. She went ashore on the South Pier, South Shields on April 2nd, 1866, and the woman and child were the first saved by South Shields or any other Volunteer Life Brigade.

South Tyneside Public Libraries and Museums

NORTH COUNTRY CLOCKMAKERS

In the 18th and early 19th century almost every town and village in Northumberland and Durham had its clockmaker, hundreds have been recorded and many specimens of their work have survived. The mass production of clocks in the second half of the 19th century put an end to this craft. It also led unfortunately to the destruction of many "grandfathers" whose cases were broken up and the brass movements melted down. This has been followed in the past 20 years by an even greater tragedy. Thousands of these memorials of our craftsmen ancestors have been exported without any opposition from the government and many millionaires have emerged from this *trade*. We can only hope that those who still possess these valuable antiques will hold on to them and pass them down within their own families.

Most of the clocks made in this area were of *long-case* or *grandfather type*. Few had the short pendulum so *bracket* or *mantlepiece* clocks are rare, likewise the larger *wall-clocks*.

Although we know the names of many clockmakers, they are recorded in old directories and newspapers, and some signed their work, the names of the case-makers are almost unknown.

When an apprentice Thomas Bewick engraved clock-dials. The work made his hands so hard and calloused that he almost gave up his training as an apprentice.

One of the best known village clockmakers was William Murray of Bellingham and later Rothbury. We have records of thirteen members of his family who followed the same trade. John Bolton of Chester-le-Street and Durham specialised in church and turret clocks but also made many fine "grandfathers". In 1771 David Hastings supplied a public clock to the town of Alnwick and in 1778 the first Newcastle Directory records twelve clockmakers as below:—

CARNABY, JOHN, East Side, Sandhill.
COVENTRY, WILLIAM, West End of the Low Bridge.
FENTON, WILLIAM, East End of Denton Chair.
GREAVES, WILLIAM, Foot of Plummer Chair, Quayside.
HARRISON, JOHN, Side.
HAWTHORN, JOHN, Pudding Chair.
PEARSON, THO., near the Vine, Flesh Market.
STOKELL, HUGH, near Painter Heugh, Pilgrim Street.
STRACHAN, ARCH., High Bridge.
TICKLE, WILLIAM, Wool Market.
WALKER, MRS., Near Castle Stairs, Close.
WILSON, JOHN, near Black Swan, Fleshmarket.

For a list of North Country Clockmakers in the 17th, 18th and 19th century see an important article by C. Leo Reid in the Archaeologia Aeliana (1925).

The bracket clock illustrated above was made by Frank Graham (no relation) Frank Graham was the last of the Newcastle Clockmakers. He died in his workshop in the Side beside his clocks, August 1855, aged 80.

Northumberland
ELECTION!!!

THE
Britannia
STEAM VESSEL,

Of 50 Horse power, will start from the Ferry-boat Landing, for Alnmouth, on Monday Morning next at half-past Five,

ARRIVE

There at Nine, and leave for her return at Six o'Clock in the Evening.

ALNMOUTH is about four Miles from Alnwick, and there are numerous Conveyances for Passengers.

FARE.—2s. 6d. Each Way.

South Shields, 23rd June, 1826.

Market Place: printed by R. M. Kelly.

A TRIP TO
Scotswood & Blaydon

The Steam Boat
VENUS

Will leave the New Quay, North Shields, at 5 o'Clock, the Ferry Boat Landing, South Shields, at half-past 5, and the Scullar Stairs, at 6, on **SUNDAY MORNING** next, the 5th August, for Scotswood and Blaydon.

Fare there and back, 1s.

Tickets to be had of MICHAEL STOREY, Wapping Street, and JAMES CLENNET, Fountain Tavern, West Holborn.

South Shields, 30th July, 1838.

Market Place Printing Offices:—R. M. Kelly, South Shields.

GRAND
TYNE REGATTA

THE MEMBERS OF THE
Jarrow Alkali Works Brass Band
Respectfully inform the Inhabitants of South and North Shields that they have engaged for the above occasion, that large and most powerful Boat of the Tyne, the

TRUMP,

Mr. JAMES BROWN, Commander.

Ladies and Gentlemen wishing to witness the grand and interesting Sport will find Accommodation in this Vessel superior to that of any other Boat in the River. The best Moorings have already been engaged for her, so that the Company can witness the Sport with Pleasure. The Members of the Band, wishing if possible to oblige all, will be most assiduous in their attentions.

The Boat will leave the Middle Dock, South Shields, a 11 o'Clock precisely. Fare only SIXPENCE.

Tickets to be had at the House of Mr. WILLIAM HIND, "Banks of the Tyne," West Holborn; and of the Members of the Band; also, of Mr. GEORGE WASCOE, and Mr. CHAPMAN, Spirit Merchant, North Shields.

South Shields, 4th August, 1843.

PASSENGER BOATS ON THE TYNE

In the 19th century and the early 20th century travel by sea both for business and pleasure was very common. On the Tyne itself numerous boats, many of them of considerable size, carried passengers. The river was a busy artery for commerce and entertainment.

Passenger traffic by steam was first introduced in England on the Tyne in 1814 (The first steam boat was first used for passengers in 1807 and on the Clyde in 1812, so the Tyne was the third place to introduce this form of passenger transport).

"On Monday afternoon at 5 o'clock," (said the *Newcastle Chronicle* on the 26th of February, 1814), "A new steam-vessel, lately built on the South Shore, near this town, was launched into the river, and called *The Tyne Steam Boat*." This little packet carried her first passengers on "The Barge Day" of the same yaer. It created a sensation and

TRIP TO
Scotswood & Blagdon

The Powerful and fast sailing Steam Vessel

VENUS

Will (weather permitting) leave
COOKSON'S QUAY, SOUTH SHIELDS,

For Scotswood and Blagdon, on

Saturday Morning, 3rd August,

At 7 o'Clock, precisely and return the same Evening,

on which occasion
Hutchinson's South Shields and Westoe

AMATEUR BAND,

will attend for the amusement of their Friends.

FARE THERE AND BACK, 1s. EACH,

An early application is advisable;

Tickets to be had Mr JOHN. HUTCHINSON, Dean Street;
of Mr ROBT. JEFFERSON, Coble Landing; Mr JOHN. THOMPSON,
Fairles' Bank: or any of the Members of the Band.

Ale, Porter, Spirits &c. at the usual Prices.

Market Place Printing Offices: R. M. Kelly, South Shields   1839

---

was the "principal novelty of the day". The *Chronicle* tells us "it followed the same track as the other part of the procession, greatly outstripping it, however, by the rapidity of its motion. The velocity with which it moves through the water, when favoured by the tide, is very great, it having run from Shields to this town, we understand, in less than an hour. Against the tide, its motion, of course, is not so rapid; but even thus impeded, it appears to move at the rate of three or four miles an hour."

On special trips at Race Week the fares were given as "best cabin, 1s.: second cabin, 6d." The following year, (9th November, 1815) it adopted the name of the *Perseverance* steam-packet.

Passenger voyages by sea started with Scottish boats in 1814. On the 10th of September, 1814, a steam boat called the *Caledonia* sailing from Dundee was the first steamer entering Shields Harbour from the sea. On her entrance we are told "she was loudly cheered".

In 1818 Joseph Price, of the Durham Glass Works, Gateshead started for the first time to tow sailing vessels to sea by steamboat. The vessels he used were the *Eagle* and *Perseverance*. The new practice was an important commercial development for the river.

The first Tyne steamer to go to sea was the small packet the *Rapid* which made voyages to London in 1823 and 1824. The venture was a commercial failure. She carried insufficient passengers and because of her size could not carry sufficient coal for the journey to London and back. She had to take on expensive coal in London. The first boat to carry passengers regularly between the Tyne and the Forth was the *Newcastle* with Joseph Fidler as Captain.

When Mackenzie wrote his history of Newcastle in 1827 he stated that up to that year forty-eight steam packets had been built on the Tyne, "ten of which were engaged at other ports or laid aside" and the remainder were plying on the river.

HOUSING IN MINING VILLAGES

The labourers in coal and other mines belong to the best paid categories of the British proletariat. The price at which they buy their wages was shown on an earlier page. Here I merely cast a hurried glance over the conditions of their dwellings. As a rule, the exploiter of a mine, whether its owner or his tenant, builds a number of cottages for his hands. They receive cottages and coal for firing "for nothing" — i.e., these form part of their wages, paid in kind. Those who are not lodged in this way receive in compensation £4 per annum. The mining districts attract with rapidity a large population, made up of the miners themselves, and the artisans, shopkeepers etc., that group themselves around them. The ground-rents are high, as they generally are where population is dense. The master tries, therefore, to run up, within the smallest space possible at the mouth of the pit, just so many cottages as are necessary to pack together his hands and their families. If new mines are opened in the neighbourhood, or old ones are again set working, the pressure increases. In the construction of the cottages, only one point of view is of moment, the "abstinence" of the capitalist from all expenditure that is not absolutely unavoidable. "The lodging which is obtained by the pitmen and other labourers connected with the collieries of Northumberland and Durham", says Dr. Julian Hunter, "is perhaps, on the whole, the worst and dearest of which any large specimins can be found in England, the similar parishes of Monmouthshire excepted . . . The extreme badness is the high number of men found in one room, in the smallness of the ground-plot on which a great number of houses are thrust, the want of water, the absence of privies, and the frequent placing of one house on the top of another, or distribution into flats, . . . the lessee acts as if the whole colony were encamped, not resident."

"In pursuance of my instructions," says Dr. Stevens, "I visited most of the large colliery villages in the Durham Union. With very few exceptions, the general statement that no means are taken to secure the health of the inhabitants would be true of all of them. All colliers are bound ('bound', an expression which, like bondage, dates from the age of serfdom) to the colliery lessee or owner for twelve months. If the colliers express discontent, or in any way annoy the 'viewer', a mark or memorandum is made against their names, and, at the annual 'binding', such men are turned off. It appears to me that no part of the 'truck system' could be worse than what obtains in these densely populated districts. The collier is bound to take as part of his hiring a house surrounded with pestiferous influences; he cannot help himself, and it appears doubtful whether anyone else can help him except his proprietor (he is, to all intents and purposes, a serf), and his proprietor first consults his balance-sheet, and the result is tolerably certain. The collier is also often supplied with water by the proprietor, which, whether it be good or bad, he has to pay for, or rather he suffers a reduction for it from his wages."

Karl Marx — Capital 1887

Colliers' Cottages Long Benton c. 1890

80

MORPETH WATCH TOWER

THE BODY SNATCHERS

In the early years of the nineteenth century there was a big demand among doctors for dead bodies required for anatomical experiments and teaching purposes. Since it became difficult to obtain enough bodies after the Napoleonic Wars were over unscrupulous people used to plunder graveyards to obtain newly buried corpses which they sold at high prices. These people were known as Resurrectionists or Body-Snatchers. To prevent this practice the graves of newly buried persons were guarded and watch towers were built in graveyards where the guards could stay. The best known is the one at Morpeth which we here depict. This was erected in 1832 when John Briggs, James Atkinson, Thomas Wilson, and Thomas Blair were churchwarders as the tablet records. A similar one can be seen in the southeast corner of the churchyard at Doddington which was built in 1826. Many churchyards were surrounded with very high railings literally to 'keep the corpses in.' An example can be seen at the top of Westgate Road in Newcastle. Many amusing, as well as macabre stories, are told about the body-snatchers. Once two of them were working one dark winter morning. A baker was passing close to the churchyard with his basket on his shoulder, when suddenly a corpse was dropped from the wall. With a yell of terror, he dropped his basket and ran at his utmost speed. The body-snatcher, thinking it was a resuscitation of the corpse, said to his mate: 'Hey, Bill, we'll hev to hev another; that yen's bolted!'

To guard their relatives when they died people used to join "Watch clubs" which gathered weekly contributions and when a member died all the others took it in turns to watch his grave. Across the border in Scotland even more elaborate precautions were taken, Heavy "iron safes" were placed on top of the graves.

EPITAPHS

Books of epitaphs are very popular but some of the best insertions are pure invention. Here are some from the North Country with no guarantee that they are genuine.

EPITAPH ON A BUTCHER

This monument here marks the spot
  Where William Thompson lies,
Who fell to instantaneous death
  A blooming sacrifice.

He in duty, as a Butcher on
  The "cratch" a Victim laid;
When duly slain, in heedless haste,
  He sheath'd the sharpen'd blade.

The sheath contained a hole, through which
  Its erring point did bound,
Pierc'd deep the pope's eye of his thigh,
  And gave a fatal wound.

Down ran the purple tide of gore
  In one continued course;
Physicians tried their skill in vain
  To stop its rapid force.

He felt his strength, his sight, his speech,
  Fast ebbing with his breath,
And on the lap of rosey health
  Sank in the sleep of death.

An eptitaph in Sunderland Parish Churchyard. A butcher's knife, steel and sheath, are sculptured on the top of the gravestone.

EPITAPH ON AN ENGINEER

My engine now is cold and still,
No water does my boiler fill;
My coke affords its flame no more,
My days of usefulness are oe'r;
My wheels deny their wanted speed,
No more my guiding hand they heed;
My whistle, too, has lost its tone,
Its shrill and thrilling sounds are gone;
My valves are now thrown open wide,
My flanges, also, refuse to guide;
My clocks, also, though once so strong,
Refuse their aid in the busy throng;
No more I feel each urging breath,
My steam is all condensed in death.
Life's railway's o'er, each stations past,
In death I'm stopped, and rest at last.
Farewell, dear friends, and cease to weep,
In Christ I'm safe — in Him I sleep.

Epitaph in Whickham Churchyard to Oswald Gardner, the driver of a locomotive engine, who lost his life in an accident near Stocksfield Station on August 15th, 1840.

Here lies ROBERT WALLIS,
The King of Good Fellows,
Clerk of All-Hallows,
And maker of bellows.
All Saints', Newcastle

Here lies the body of Thomas Kemp,
  Who lived by wool and died by hemp;
There's nothing would suffice this glutton,
  But with the fleece to steal the mutton;
Had he but worked and lived uprighter,
  He'd ne'er been hung for a sheep-biter.
Bellingham Churchyard

Here lies the remains of L. GEDGE, Printer,
Like a worn-out character, he has returned to the
  Founder,
Hoping that he will be re-cast in a better and more
  perfect mould.
Morpeth Parish Churchyard

Stop passenger for here is laid,
  One who the debt of nature paid.
This is not strange, the reader cries,
  We all know here a dead man lies.
You're right; but stop I'll tell you more:
  He never paid a debt before;
And now he's gone, I'll further say,
  He never will another pay.
Corbridge Parish Churchyard

Here lies WALTER GUNN,
Sometimes landlord of the Tun;
Sic transot gloria mundi!
He drank hard upon Friday
That being a high day,
Then took to his bed and died upon Sunday.
Blyth Cemetery

Eliza, sorrowing
Reads this marble slab
To her dear John
Who died of eating crab.
Consett Cemetery

82

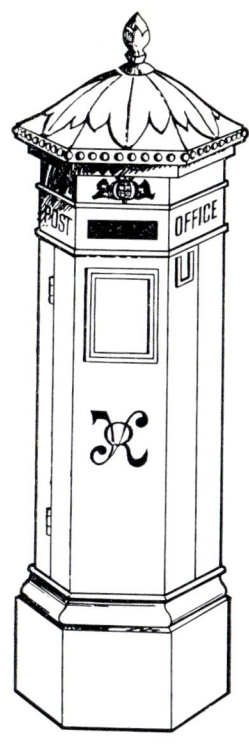

Letter Box in Osborne Avenue, Newcastle.

OLD LETTER BOXES

In Osborne Avenue, Jesmond, Newcastle there is a fine pillar box, the oldest in Northumberland. It is first recorded in June, 1884, and has probably already celebrated its centenary. Before the introduction of letter boxes in Newcastle and before letters were delivered by postmen letters "to be called for" were "exposed in the window" of the Quayside Post Office. The letters then were mostly for captains and crews of the sailing vessels which visited Newcastle.

The first letter boxes, six-sided pillar boxes were set up on the island of Guernsey. The famous novelist Anthony Trollope had suggested them when he was a Post Office Surveyor's Clerk. The first recorded letter box in Northumberland was installed in a wall at Corbridge Railway Station on February 10th, 1882. Records do not go back beyond 1882 but it is very unlikely that the north east had to wait 30 years for this service. Letter boxes were in use in Elswick Road, Newcastle (June 1882) Bentinck Road, Newcastle (July 1883), The Grove, Gosforth (June 1883) and the still existing Osborne Avenue in June, 1884.

At first every area designed its own letter boxes and it wasn't until 1859 that standard national pillar boxes were introduced. They were plain in design and rounded. None have survived in our area.

Between 1866-1879 hexagonal letter boxes were introduced. They were called *Penfolds* after their designer Mr. J. W. Penfold. During this period the design was modified slightly three times. The one in Osborne Avenue is the third type and so must have been erected between 1872 and 1879.

DICKENS IN THE NORTH

On the 1st February, 1838, Charles Dickens put up at the King's Head situated in the Market Place of Barnard Castle and here he stayed for two days. He had come north to gather information about the Yorkshire schools, which formed the background to his novel "Nicholas Nickleby".

The inn has been enlarged since Dickens' visit but the older portion in which he stayed "has been preserved and remains much as it was, with the same antique staircase, the same low-ceilinged rooms, the same Georgian fireplaces and the same small-panel windows".

Dickens was well satisfied with his quarters at the King's Head and he has immortalised the hostelry in "Nicholas Nickleby". Just as he was leaving the Saracen's Head in London for Yorkshire Nicholas was given a letter by the eccentric Newman Noggs with instructions to read it when alone. At the end of the letter were these words

"P.S. If you should go near Barnard Castle, there is good ale at the King's Head. Say you know me and I am sure they will not charge you for it. You may say Mr. Noggs there, for I was a gentleman then, I was indeed."

The inn is of the Georgian period and was built about the middle of the 18th century. The first landlord we read of was Robert Wood in 1792. At the beginning of the 19th century the licensee was Richard Harrison, and it remained in his family until 1906. When Dickens stayed there the landlord was Henry Ewbank who had married one of Harrison's two daughters. The two sisters used to tell visitors that Dickens wrote a good deal of "Nicholas Nickleby" in their house. He was always writing it was

of the impressions he received. His first visit was to Newcastle, on August 27th, 1852, when along with others he acted in the Assembly Rooms in behalf of the 'Guild of Literature and Art.' The next day he acted in Sunderland from whence he wrote to John Forster on August 29th.

"Into the room at Newcastle they squeezed six hundred people, at twelve and sixpence, into a space reasonably capable of holding three hundred. Last night, in a hall built like a theatre, The Lyceum in Lambton Street, with pit, boxes, and gallery, we had about twelve hundred—dare say more. They began with a round of applause when Coote's white waistcoat appeared in the orchestra, and wound up the farce with three deafening cheers. I never saw such good fellows. Stanny is their fellow-townsman; was born here; and they applauded his scene as if it were himself. But what I suffered from a dreadful anxiety that hung over me all the time, I can never describe. When we got here at noon, it appeared that the hall was a perfectly new one, and had only had the slates put upon the roof by torchlight over night. Further, that the proprietors of some opposition rooms had declared the building to be unsafe, and that there was a panic in the town about it; people having had their money back, and being undecided whether to come or not, and all kinds of such horrors. I didn't know what to do. The horrible responsibility of risking an accident of that awful nature seemed to rest upon me; for I had only to say we wouldn't act, and there would be no chance of danger. I was afraid to take Sloman into council lest the panic should infect our men. I asked W. what he thought, and he consolingly observed that his digestion was so bad that death had no terrors for him!

said and they could show the ink-stand he used during the stay there. The story is of course exaggerated. He only stayed two days not the six weeks usually claimed.

"It was whilst on this short visit that Dickens made the acquaintance of Mr. Humphrey, who kept a watchmaker's shop lower down the street. This worthy conducted him to some of the schools in the neighbourhood, and from the friendly association, sprang the title of Master Humphrey's Clock, used by the novelist for his next serial. When Dickens first met Mr. Humphrey, who we believe was the source from which sprang all the legendary stories about Dickens and Barnard Castle, he exhibited no clock outside his shop. It was not until two years after Dickens's visit that the old man, having moved opposite the inn, placed a clock above the door". (B. W. Matz).

Charles Dickens visited the North on four more occasions, and in his letters gave interesting and humorous accounts

Master Humphrey's Shop Amen Corner Barnard Castle P/G

I went and looked at the place; at the rafters, walls, pillars, and so forth; and fretted myself into a belief that they really were slight! To crown all, there was an arched iron roof without any brackets or pillars, on a new principle! The only comfort I had was in stumbling at length on the builder, and finding him a plain practical north-countryman with a foot rule in his pocket. I took him aside, and asked him should we, or could we, prop up any weak part of the place: especially the dressing rooms, which were under our stage, the weight of which must be heavy on a new floor, and dripping wet walls. He told me there wasn't a stronger building in the world; and that, to allay the apprehension, they had opened it, on Thursday night, to thousands of the working people, and induced them to sing, and beat with their feet, and make every possible trial of the vibration. Accordingly there was nothing for it but to go on. I was in such dread, however, lest a false alarm should spring up among the audience and occasion a rush, that I kept Catherine and Georgina out of the front. When the curtain went up and I saw the great sea of faces rolling up to the roof, I looked here and looked there, and thought I saw the gallery out of the perpendicular, and fancied the lights in the ceiling were not straight. Rounds of applause were perfect agony to me, I was so afraid of their effect upon the building. I was ready all night to rush on in case of alarm — a false alarm was my main dread — and implore the people for God's sake to sit still. I had our great-farce bell rung to startle Sir Geoffrey instead of throwing down a piece of wood, which might have raised a sudden apprehension. I had a palpitation of the heart, if any of our people stumbled up or down a stair. I am sure I never acted better, but the anxiety of my mind was so intense, and the relief at last so great, that I am half-dead today, and have not yet been able to eat or drink anything or to stir out of my room. I shall never forget it. As to the short time we had for getting the theatre up; as to the upsetting, by a runaway pair of horses, of one of the vans at the Newcastle railway station with all the scenery in it, every atom of which was turned over; as to the fatigue of our carpenters, who have now been up four nights, and who were lying dead asleep in the entrances last night, I say nothing, after the other gigantic nightmare, except that Sloman's splendid knowledge of his business, and the good temper and cheerfulness of all the workmen, are capital."

He next visited Newcastle on the 24th and 25th September, 1858, and gave three of his public readings in the Town Hall. His visit to Sunderland on this occasion was more auspicious. Writing from the Station Hotel, Newcastle, on September 26th to Miss Hogarth he says:

"Remembering what you do of Sunderland, you will be surprised that our profit there was very considerable. I read in a beautiful new theatre, and (I thought to myself) quite wonderfully. Such an audience I never beheld for rapidity and (converted into a theatre afterwards) was burnt to the ground a year or two ago. We found the hotel, so bad in our time, really good. I

walked from Durham to Sunderland, and from Sunderland to Newcastle."

In 1861 Dickens was again in Newcastle and gave three readings in the Music Hall, Nelson Street on the 21st, 22nd and 23rd November. The first reading was poorly attended, due to an oversight in the advertising, although "the audience was the most enthusiastic and appreciative imaginable," but the second night was a success. Writing to Forster he says:

"At Newcastle, against the very heavy expenses, I made more than a hundred guineas profit. A finer audience there is not in England, and I suppose them to be a specially earnest people; for, while they can laugh till they shake the roof, they have a very unusual sympathy with what is pathetic or passionate."

In a letter to his daughter, as well as in the one above to Forster, he describes an alarming incident which took place at this reading:

"A most tremendous hall here last night; something almost terrible in the cram. A fearful thing might have happened. Suddenly, when they were all very still over Smike, my gas batten came down, and it looked as if the room was falling. There were three great galleries crammed to the roof, and a high steep flight of stairs, and a panic must have destroyed numbers of people. A lady in the front row of stalls screamed, and ran out wildly towards me, and for one instant there was a terrible wave in the crowd. I addressed that lady laughing (for I knew she was in sight of everybody there), and called out as if it happened every night, 'There's nothing the matter, I assure you; don't be alarmed; pray sit down;' and she sat down directly, and there was a thunder of applause. It took some few minutes to mend, and I looked on with my hands in my pockets; for I think if I had turned my back for a moment there might still have been a move. My people were dreadfully alarmed, Boylett in particular, who I suppose had some notion that the whole place might have taken fire."

From Newcastle he travelled to Berwick, in very stormy weather, and an hour before his reading there, he wrote from the King's Arms:

"An odd and out of the way a place to be at, it appears to me, as ever was seen! And such a ridiculous room designed for me to read in! An immense Corn Exchange, made of glass and iron, round, dome-topp'd, lofty, utterly absurd for any such purpose, and full of thundering echoes; with a little lofty crow's nest of a stone gallery, breast high, deep in the wall, into which it was designed to put——me! I instantly struck, of course; and said I would either read in a room attached to this house (a very snug one, capable of holding 500 people), or not at all. Terrified local agents glowered, but fell prostrate, and my men took the primitive accomodation in hand. Ever since, I am alarmed to add, the people (who besought the honour of the visit) have been coming in numbers quite irreconcilable with the appearance of the place, and what is to be the end I do not know. It

41·GREY·STREET

Ball Room at the Kings Arms Hotel, Berwick.

was poor Arthur Smith's principle that a town on the way paid the expenses of a long through-journey, and therefore I came."

His last visit to Newcastle was in the first week in March, once again in the Music Hall, with three readings. Writing to Miss Hogarth he gives a fine compliment to the people of Newcastle:

"The readings have made an immense effect in this place, and it is remarkable that although the people are individually rough, collectively they are an unusually tender and sympathetic audience; while their comic perception is quite up to the high London standard. The atmosphere is so very heavy that yesterday we escaped to Tynemouth for a two hours' sea walk. There was a high north wind blowing and a magnificent sea running. Large vessels were being towed in and out over the stormy bar, with prodigious waves breaking on it; and spanning the restless uproar of the waters was a quiet rainbow of transcendent beauty. The scene was quite wonderful. We were in the full enjoyment of it when a heavy sea caught us, knocked us over, and in a moment drenched us, and filled even our pockets. We had nothing for it but to shake ourselves together (like Doctor Marigold) and dry ourselves as well as we could by hard walking in the wind and sunshine! But we were wet through for all that when we came back here to dinner after an hour's railway ride."

BILLY PURVIS

The Music halls of the North produced many fine comedians in the 19th and early 20th centuries. None was so famous nor so well remembered as Billy Purvis who was born in 1784 and for almost fifty years his booth was the centre of attraction at fairs, hoppings and feasts between Tweed and Tees. He was born across the Border in Scotland but when he was two his parents moved to Newcastle to a house in the Close which was to remain Billy's "home" till the day he died.

He was apprenticed to a joiner and when his apprenticeship was completed he worked at his trade for a number of years. He early showed an interest in acting and was the manager of a band cf amateur performers at the *St. George and Dragon* in Gateshead. While still working at his trade he undertook acting work of every kind. He was the "fool" at a show on the Town Moor during Race Week, a drum-major in the Hexham Militia, and a dancing master. He learnt the art of legerdemain from travelling conjurors and magicians and became a fine performer on the pipes. He had meanwhile been "sacked" from his work as a joiner.

In 1819 he became the owner of a booth and launched out as a travelling theatre owner. For years he was now travelling the "northern circuit", visiting places where today no entertainment at all is available. The story of his life by J. R. Robson, the Newcastle poet, provides us with a most interesting account of Billy's adventures as he toured the north with his theatre. The entertainer of those times had to be versatile and Billy Purvis was a conjurer, singer, dancer, comedian, actor, puppeter and many other things besides.

One of the most popular of Billy's acts which made him famous, was "stealing the bundle" illustrated above.

"It was a rare treat to see Billy steal the bundle. It was never the same thing twice. The drollery was always fresh. The discovery of the bundle—the speculations as to who it belonged to—what might be its contents—whether it wold be safe to open it—whether it really had or had not an owner—whether the man or woman who laid it there had not stolen in, or forgotten it, or thrown it away because tired of carrying it—whether the owner would ever come back for it—whether, if he stole it, he would be detected—whether there was, after all, such a thing as stealing—whether every appropriation of a thing was not stealing—whether one could be said to steal a bundle like that when no one seemed to have any better claim to it—what he would do if he took and opened the bundle, and found to contents to be so and so, as tobacco, groceries, clothes, or something else—all this monologue or soliloquy, delivered in the purest Tyneside vernacular, with irresistibly comic manual and facial action and broad local and personal allusions, was certain to bring down the house. And, then, when at length he did 'lowse' the bundle, what revelations! As Billy's amanuensis and editor, J. P. Robson, says, in a clever song he wrote on the subject, which was sung to the tune of 'The King of the Canibal Islands', he could coax dumplings from an old wife's pan, turn tea to blacking, sugar to chalk, girdle cakes to half bricks, and bring them promiscuously out of his marvellous bundle, making his audiences 'fit to pull doon a' the playce'."

Billy died at Hartlepool on December 16th, 1853 and is buried in St. Hilda's Churchyard.

BILLY AS A CLOWN.

BILLY AND HIS PIPES.

STEALING THE BUNDLE.

THE BONNY MOOR HEN

In the Market Square at Stanhope stand two inns, the 'Packhorse', once the Stanhope coach terminus, and the 'Phoenix' Hotel, built by Frederick Fenwick who used the family crest as a sign. The 'Phoenix' stands on the site of the 'Black Bull Inn', the scene of the fight known as the Battle of Stanhope.

It all started in 1797 when the Bishop of Durham issued a notice against poachers on his moors, a proclamation which was defied by the men of Weardale who considered hunting one of their immemorial rights. At last in 1818 a large body of the Bishop's men came into Weardale to arrest the best known among the poachers, boasting they "could sweep Weardale with a black pudding". Two poachers were arrested and the Bishop's men took them to the 'Black Bull' Inn. News of the arrests quickly spread, a large crowd gathered, and a fierce battle broke out. The Bishop's men were completely routed. Many keepers and constables were severely injured and the inn floor was covered with blood which one of the poachers told the landlady "to mix with meal and make black pudding of it".

The story of this affray was related in a ballad called "The Bonny Moor Hen", written, it is believed, by a local schoolmaster:

THE BONNY MOOR HEN

You brave lads of Weardale, I pray lend an ear,
The account of a battle you quickly shall hear,
That was fought by the miners, so well you may ken,
By claiming a right to their bonny moor hen.

Oh this bonny moor hen, as it plainly appears,
She belonged to their fathers some hundreds of years;
But the miners of Weardale are all valiant men,
They will fight till they die for their bonny moor hen.

These industrious miners that walk in their clogs,
They suit them to travel o'er mountains and bogs;
When the bonny moor hen she mounts up in the air,
They will bring her down neatly, I vow and declare.

Oh the miners in Weardale, they are bred to the game,
They level their pieces and make sure of their aim;
When the shot it goes off—Oh, the powder doth sing,
They are sure to take off, either a leg or a wing.

Now, the times being hard and provisions being dear,
The miners were starving almost we do hear;
They had nought to depend on, so well you may ken,
But to make what they could of the bonny moor hen.

There's the fat man of Oakland, and Durham the same,
Lay claim to the moors, likewise to the game;
They sent word to the miners they'd have them to ken
They would stop them from shooting the bonny moor hen.

Oh these words they were carried to Weardale with speed,
Which made the poor miners to hang down their heads;
But sent them an answer, they would have them to ken,
They would fight till they died for their bonny moor hen.

When this answer it came to the gentlemen's ears,
An army was risen, it quickly appears;
Land-stewards, bum-bailiffs, and game-keepers too,
Were all ordered to Weardale to fight their way through.

A captain was wanted at the head of the clan;
H. Wye, of great Oakland was chose for their man;
Oh, his legs were too small, and not fit for the stocks,
His scalp not being hard for to suffer the knocks.

Oh, this captain he had a black bitch of his own,
That was taught by the master 'twas very well known;
By the help of his bitch he'd met many a one,
And when he comes to Weardale he'll do what he can.

"Oh," this captain says, "I am but a stranger here,
My bitch and myself is a match for a deer;
Either beggars or tinkers, she will pull off their bags,
And if that will not do she will rive them to rags."

So this army set out from high Oakland, we hear,
H. Wye in the front, and black bitch in the rear;
On they marched to Wolsingham, then made a halt,
And concerning the battle began to consult.

They heard that the miners' grand army was strong,
The captain that led them was full six feet long;
That put Mr. Wye in a bodily fear,
And back to great Oakland he wish'd for to steer.

Up spoke the game-keepers: "Cheer up, never fear,
Through Stanhope and Weardale our way we will clear;
In Durham or Oakland it shall never be said,
That by a few miners our army was paid."

So the army set off straightway, as we hear,
And the miners' grand army did quickly appear;
Oh, they fired along till their powder was done,
And then they laid on with the butt-end of their guns.

They dismounted the riders staightway on the plain,
H. Wye and black bitch in the battle were slain;
Oh they that ran fastest got first out of town,
And away they went home with their tails hanging down.

Oh this battle was fought all in Stanhope town,
When the chimneys did reek and the soot it fell down;
Such a battle was ne'er fought in Stanhope before,
And I hope such a battle will ne'er be fought more.

Oh this bonny moor hen, she's gone oe'r the plain,
When summer comes back she'll return here again;
They will tip her so neatly, that no one'll ken,
That ever they rivall'd the bonny moor hen.

Oh this bonny moor hen, she has feathers anew,
She has many fine colours, but none of them blue;
Oh the miners of Weardale, they are all valiant men,
They will fight till they die for the bonny moor hen.

The old poaching song is still popular in Weardale. The "Battle of Stanhope" and the subsequent troubles led in 1820 to the founding of a protection society known as the "Association for the Prosecution of Felons and other Offenders", which still survives as a social club, meeting annually in the old 'King's Arms' at St. John's Chapel. At that time St. John's Chapel was a flourishing place. The Weardale lead mines were flourishing, the population was growing and there was plenty of money about. Drink was cheap and drunkeness was common. There was no real police force so a society to preserve law and order had strong support. Meetings are still held at the King's Arms but today it is only a society of elderly people who meet for a convivial evening.

✿ ✿ SOUVENIR ✿ ✿

Opening of South Shields Electric Tramways,
March 30th, 1906.